Coal in the Blood

Coal Mining in Stanley & District

by
Jack Hair

Hedley Pit boilers during the 1920s strike. The officials had to work and maintain the boilers so as to avoid permanent damage.

Previous page: Five miners underground at Burnhope Colliery. They were: Jack Thompson, Tommy Walters, John Bradley, Ken Lumley and Andrew Heslop. This was the only colliery in the district where the boilers were underground.

Front cover: My great-grandfather Jonathan Lambert – a Burns Pit miner.

Copyright © Jack Hair 2009

First published in 2009 by

Summerhill Books
PO Box 1210
Newcastle-upon-Tyne
NE99 4AH

Email: andrew_clark@hotmail.co.uk

ISBN: 978-1-906721-12-1

Printed by: CVN Print, Maxwell Street, South Shields

Contents

Introduction	4
Andrews House Colliery	5
Annfield Plain – Lizzie Pit, South Pontop Colliery	6
Annfield Plain – Willie Pit, South Derwent Colliery	7
Tommy Armstrong – The Pitman's Poet	8
Beamish Collieries – Beamish Mary, Air and Second Pit	10
John Buddle	13
Burnhope Collieries	14
Burnopfield Colliery – The Hobson	16
Byermoor Colliery	18
Causey Arch	20
Craghead Collieries	22
Charlie Pit – New Shield Row Colliery	26
Dipton Delight Pit	27
East Castle	29
East Pontop Colliery	29
East Stanley Colliery (Jackie's Pit)	30
East Tanfield and Causey Mill Drift	31
Handon Hold Colliery	34
Pontop Colliery	34
High Stables Colliery, South Medomsley	35
Lord James Joicey	38
Kibblesworth Colliery	39
Lintz Colliery – Anna and Billy Pits	40
Louisa Colliery	41
Marley Hill Colliery	44
Miners' Sunday	49
Morrison Collieries – North and Busty	50
John Pattison – East Stanley Poet	64
Oakey's Pit, West Shield Row Colliery	65
Shield Row Drift	66
Stanhope and Tyne Railway	68
South Tanfield Colliery, Oxhill	69
Tanfield Moor Colliery	70
Tanfield Lea Colliery	71
West Stanley Colliery (The Burns Pit)	75
William Pit, Old South Moor	88
Hedley Colliery, South Moor	90
Tanfield Railway	96
A Selection of Mining Poetry	98
The Colliery Welfare	101
The Disgrace of Coal and Stone Dust	102
Acknowledgements	104

Introduction

This is a book of the coal mining industry in Stanley & District, North Durham. It does not include every mine, as in the early days, there were many small drift mines and bell pits around the area. I have no photos of these, but do mention a few of them. The book is also only a reflection of the coal mining industry in the way of memories, rather than a purely factual historic account, and I make no apology for this. If what you need is facts and figures, then go to the Records Office, Museum, or Mining Institutes. Even here, the many experts give varying accounts of the same subject. I can't be the judge as to which of them is correct. The book also reflects the huge cost paid by the miners in this truly dangerous occupation.

My history interest over the last six books has been the involvement of talking to people and reflecting their memories. These people have lived our history. They are the experts, and I feel a richer person for having met them. My only sadness, is that it has come to an end. My poor health, and deteriorating eyesight make research almost impossible.

If my efforts in writing books, giving talks and slideshows have encouraged others to take an interest in local history, then it will all have been worthwhile. I would advise anyone to sit quietly for a while, and write down their memories as far back as they can remember. It is very therapeutic, and brings back thoughts long forgotten.

I am retaining my website, and you are invited to visit at any time, and share a few moments looking back. Thank you for your support over the years.

My website is: www.stanley-codurham-jackhair.com

Jack Hair
Stanley, 2009

An aerial photograph of Stanley.

Andrews House Colliery

This colliery was situated near the Causey Arch, and was opened in 1843 by John Bowes & Ptnrs. Most of the men employed lived near the colliery, (see map). Up until 1896, the output was only coal but from that year coking and gas were introduced. By 1914, there were almost 300 men employed there. During the harvest period on the farms nearby, the men sometimes worked and were given an extra bonus for their efforts. The colliery closed in December 1920.

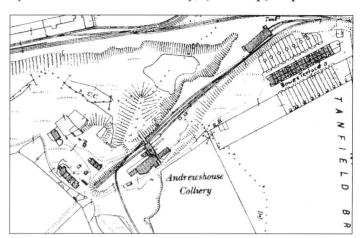

Right: A map of Andrews House Colliery. The houses to the right were named Bowes Terrace.

Miners' Flit

Miners and their families travelled to the district from all over Britain, with a particular large number from Devon and Cornwall. The mixture of languages came together into what is known as "Pitmatic". This is very similar to Geordie, but a little less harsh. Even this has derivations from village to village. For example, in Stanley, they would say "Craghead", yet in Craghead, they would say "Cragheed". Another one is Sacriston, pronounced as it is spelt in the Stanley area, yet some others pronounce it as "Seggison". Sometimes, while I have worked away from home, others have likened my speech as Welsh and people have said we definitely have a

different sound than Geordie. The family shown have all their possessions on the cart, and are supposedly doing a moonlight flit. Many of them were signed up on contract and were unable to leave without the permission of the coal owner.

Annfield Plain – Lizzie Pit South Pontop Colliery

The Lizzie Pit was situated in the Greencroft area of Annfield Plain. There are references to this colliery in the 1860s but I do not have a year of opening. It closed in April 1927. The highest number employed was in 1902 with 325 men and boys. The Ritson's were the owners most listed. Next to the colliery was Lizzie Square where many of the employees lived. One of these houses had the living room converted into a Methodist Chapel with a simple preacher's box and a few bench type seats.

The colliery worked the Hutton, Brass Thill, Five Quarter, and Shield Row seams. There is a mention of a death in 1841 when the Colliery Viewer, Edward Barnabus Smith, aged only 21, fell down the shaft. Another shaft death was that of 13 years old John Tucker in 1894. He fell from one of the shaft mouthings onto the top of the cage, a distance of 75 feet.

Left: A sketch of the Lizzie Pit Lodge at the Durham Miners' Gala.

Below: South Pontop miners at the Lizzie Pit.

Annfield Plain – Willy Pit
South Derwent Colliery

This colliery consisted of: the Cresswell Pit, the Furnace Pit, the Hutton Pit and the Willie Pit. The main owners were: Bainbridge, Kissop & Co, R. Dickinson & Co and South Derwent Coal Co. The highest employment figures seem to be 1896 with almost 500 men and boys employed. This colliery had natural drainage. Many of the men lived in Pontop Rows, Annfield Plain and the Willie Pit Cottages. These were very basic houses and at Pontop Rows, in the early days, the sewage ran down the backs of the street to the lowest level. Living conditions were described as appalling, and diseases such as cholera existed. Pontop Rows were originally erected for the railway workers of the Stanhope & Tyne Railway, which later changed its name to the Pontop & Shields Railway.

Right: South Derwent Colliery Prize Band.

Below: South Derwent Colliery officials (Willie Pit). The traditional deputy's stick was actually a measuring stick.

Above: Pontop Rows, Annfield Plain.

Tommy Armstrong
The Pitman's Poet

Tommy Armstrong wrote many poems and songs reflecting on the life and times he lived in, and the events of the day.

There are conflicting accounts of how he came to the Stanley area, and I am not sure which is which. I therefore give what information I have at the time of writing. Fred Wade says in his book of Stanley that Armstrong moved to South Pontop (Greencroft) aged 15 in 1864, and it was about this time he wrote his first song. He soon became an entertainer singing at local halls and charity events. He was very popular and surprisingly at that time could not read music. His song, *Durham Jail,* was sung by Tommy Gray at Newcastle Oxford Music Hall and won the singer a gold medal for the best pitman's singer in Northumberland and Durham.

One of Tommy's favourite songs was *The Row In The Gutter*. The gutter was an open channel that ran the full length of the colliery rows, into which each housewife poured her dirty water, which ran into a sink at the end of the row. The women of the street would often argue as to who's turn it was to clean the sink. These fallouts were very colourful with all the street turning out to listen to the arguments.

In 1866, Tommy was arrested at Addison Colliery near Blaydon. Three police officers took him out of his bed. He had apparently written some verse for funeral cards for a travelling trader who, in turn, would print and frame these poems for sale. Tommy had found out the trader had been charging more for them than had been agreed. The next time they met, he made the old man believe he was going to kill him. Tommy frightened him so much, he went to the police and reported him. A warrant was taken out for his arrest and he was remanded in Blaydon for three days, then released.

I write later in the book of the Oakey's Pit story of him being charged for defamation of character by Maiden Law Joe, due to his song *Oakey's Keeker*. This case was laughed out of court. He could very probably have made a good living with his poems, songs and entertaining, but he worked for many years as a coal hewer at Oakey's Pit. It was from this life he got most of his inspiration.

Much of his music was printed onto penny sheet and sung all over the district by local people. He was very, very popular. His songs were sung in the pitmatic dialect, and for some years, almost disappeared. However, his songs and poems seem more popular now than ever. I was at the Lamplight Theatre recently and heard several renditions of his verse and music by local artists.

After leaving South Pontop, he spent the rest of his life at Tanfield Lea (Tantobie). He died on the 30th August 1930, at Havelock Terrace, Tantobie, and was buried at Tanfield.

Other accounts say he was born at Wood Street, Shotley Bridge in 1848, where, at the age of 15, he began work as a trapper at East Tanfield Colliery. He supposedly had to be carried to work because he could hardly walk due to having rickets as a child. Yet another account says he moved to Tanfield via South Pontop and began work at the age of nine.

His brother said Tommy was born at Shotley Bridge in 1848, and moved to Annfield Plain in 1864. He and his three brothers moved to work at East Tanfield in 1886 where he worked for a number of years. He had fourteen children.

The Durham Lock Out

This song by Tommy Armstrong was written during the 1892 Durham Lock Out.
The miners had been locked out by the coal owners when they refused a wage cut.

In our Durham County, I am sorry for to say
That hunger and starvation is increasing every day;
For the want of food and coals we know not what to do,
But with your kind assistance, we will stand the struggle through.
I need not state the reason why we have been brought so low.
The masters have behaved unkind, which everyone will know;
Because we won't lie down and let them treat us as they like,
To punish us they've stopped their pits and caused the present strike.

Chorus:

May every Durham colliery owner that is in the fault,
Receive nine lashes with the rod, then be rubbed with salt.
May his back end be thick with boils, so that he cannot sit,
And never burst until the wheels go round at every pit.

The pulley wheels have ceased to move, which went so swift around.
The horses and the ponies too are brought from underground;
Our work is taken from us now, they care not if we die,
For they can eat the best of food, and drink the best when dry.
The miner, and his partner too, each morning have to roam
To seek for bread to feed, the little hungry ones at home;
The flour barrel is empty now, their true and faithful friend
Which makes the thousands wish today the strike was at an end.

We have done our very best as honest working men,
To let the pits commence again we've offered to them 'ten'.
The offer they will not accept, they firmly do demand
Thirteen and a half per cent, or let their collieries stand.
Let them stand, or let them lie, to do with them as they choose,
To give them thirteen and a half, we ever shall refuse.
They're always willing to receive, but not inclined to give,
Very soon they won't allow a working man to live.

With tyranny and capital they never seem content,
Unless they are endeavouring to take from us per cent;
If it was due what they request, we willingly would grant;
We know it's not therefore we cannot give them what they want.
The miners of Northumberland we shall for ever praise,
For being so kind in helping us those tyrannising days;
We thank the other counties too, that have been doing the same
For every man who reads will know that we are not to blame.

Although some of his songs are over a hundred years ago they are still just as popular today. There is a Tommy Armstrong Society whose website is:

www.pitmanpoet.derwentside.org.uk

Beamish Collieries
Beamish Mary, Air and Second Pit

The first of the Beamish Collieries opened in 1763 and the colliery finally closed in 1966. The Edge Pit was sunk in 1763. The Second Pit opened in 1784 and closed in 1962. There were a sequence of collieries on the south side, some named and others only a number. The Fifth Pit and Sixth Pit were also sunk in 1784. The Air Pit opened in 1849 and the Mary Pit opened in 1883.

This series of collieries were an industry of their own with farms, sawmills, warehouses and housing stock. Trees were hauled out of the local woods for pit props and other uses. Stone was quarried locally for the miners' houses, although the first stones removed from the pits was also used for this purpose. The extensive storehouses were used to store all the items needed to operate this large industrial undertaking.

There is an excellent account of this in Jack Edgell's notes of his time working for Beamish Colliery. I have a copy of these notes.

The best known of the owners were: Sir J. Eden, John Morton Davison, James Joicey, Lambton, Hetton & Joicey and the NCB.

The largest number of employees seems to have been in 1914 with a total of 1,309. There was access to Beamish Collieries from Beamish, No Place, the View Woods and Shield Row. My father and grandfather both worked there for sometime.

W. Nicholson Winderman at Beamish Colliery in 1948.

Beamish Mary Staff, 1898. The miner crouching fourth from the right is Jack Wears, father of Syd Wears Snr the former butcher from High Street, Stanley. Jack became Landlord of the Stanley Inn on the day of the Burns Pit Disaster in February 1909.

Beamish Colliery.

Beamish 2nd Pit vertical winding engine.

Right: Beamish Colliery after restructure.

My father, Billy Hair, worked at this colliery. Sometime in the early 1940s, there was a strike against introducing windy picks. The strike failed. My Dad had to abide by the strike but he received no wages during this time. When they again talked of strike, he had had enough. When things settled down he moved to East Tanfield Colliery. At this time we lived in Railway Terrace, Shield Row. This was a tied house to Beamish Colliery. Both

they and East Tanfield were owned by the same company. Regardless, we were made to leave this house with the threat of eviction. So much for the good old days. The Manager at East Tanfield obtained a flat for us at Delacour Street, Stanley.

Beamish Air Pit Lodge and Officials in the 1950s. Front row: F. Cornforth, J. Madden, W. Harrison, J. Clark, J. Main, R. Rowlands. Back row: N. Benfold, R. Muncaster, S. Shield, A. Whittaker, T. Benfold, B. Chapman, J. Dodds. Tommy Benfold was for many years Treasurer of Stanley Victoria Club & Institute and was a family friend of ours.

Pictured here is my old friend Chris Armstrong (left) standing beside the Beamish Lodge Banner. Chris played bass drum for Beamish and many other colliery bands. He also played in dance bands throughout the area. He was born in Office Row, Burnhope within yards of the colliery there. He worked there for many years before transferring to Beamish as engine winder man. He was a fervent Sunderland supporter and suffered Newcastle supporters very badly. In recent years, he moved with wife Mary to Devon.

John Buddle

John Buddle was a well renowned colliery viewer and mining engineer. He was born in Kyo, near Tanfield in County Durham on 15th September 1773. His father was at that time listed as a schoolmaster at a private school in Kyo. In 1792, his father, also named John took over as manager at Wallsend Colliery and young John, then aged 19 became his assistant. He had a very scientific mind and continuously thought of ways of improving the workings of coal mines and other things.

On the death of his father in 1796, he took over as viewer and manager of Wallsend Colliery and other workings of Mr Russell where he remained for most of his life. He also took part in many other collieries and owners business, particularly in sinkings and borings and there is a huge list of collieries he was involved with over the years. He was instrumental in improving ventilation and introduced the Davy Lamp into the local mines.

He was also involved in railways and general engineering. As he grew older he became the proprietor of coal mines as well as land, shipping and other businesses. He assisted the Marquis of Londonderry in the formation and completion of Seaham Harbour, and was present at its opening when the first coals were shipped in one of his vessels.

John Buddle died at his Wallsend residence on 10th October 1843 in his 70th year (although another obituary states 10th August 1843). He was interred at Benwell on 16th October. There was a huge procession at his funeral with up to 60 gentlemen on horseback followed by an array of carriages. He left a fortune in excess of £150,000 which in that time was a lot of money for a boy from Kyo.

Jack Thompson – Local Poet of the 20th Century

My friend Jack Thompson is a modern day poet reflecting the life around our area in his poems. In his book *Looking Back* are over 30 such poems. Having been a coal miner himself, and lived around the pit heads, life has left its scars, some of which are reflected in his work. He was made redundant at the Louisa Colliery in the early 1950s and it was later made clear to him that things would not be easy for him to return to the industry.

He later spent several years in the vehicle building industry as a trade union officer before moving into local politics where he served for many years as a county councillor. He has been a member of Annfield Plain Gleemen Male Voice Choir for many years and his other hobbies are gardening, music and helping around the house. His poetry reflects his experiences and observations from childhood to old age.

His latest book, 'Looking Back' is in the North East Poetry Series
ISBN 978-0-9555153-7-8

Burnhope Collieries

There have been several collieries at Burnhope village. These include: the Annie Pit (sunk and opened in 1850), the Betty Pit, the Engine Pit, the Fell Pit (sunk in 1893), the Fortune Pit and the Ralph Pit. The two best known owners were Ritson and the Bear Park Coal Co apart from the NCB. Coal mined from the Busty Seam was excellent coking coal while coal from the Harvey, Hutton and Low Main and Five Quarter were used for gas production.

There is also mention of several drift mines, namely, the Warren, Polo and Lanchester.

The highest employment was in 1921 with 1,023 miners.

There was an incident at the Fell Pit in 1893 when the rope snapped and the cage plunged down the shaft killing four men. They were: G. Holt, A. Laycock, J. Hall and G. Shaw.

There was a Parish Church in the village plus two Methodist Churches. There was also a school.

Above: The Burnhope Annie Pit.

Left: Burnhope Colliery bank hands, including: George Jackson, Billy Wilson, E. Bailey, W. Bennett, Isaac Rushton, Jack Souter, Bunty Smith, Matt Gray, Tommy Laverick and J.R. Smith Jnr.

After closure around 1950 many men moved to other collieries while some moved out of the village altogether. It seemed doomed for a while, but as miners adjusted to employment out of the coal industry, the village survived and is now a pleasant village only a few miles out of Durham City, surrounded by farms and beautiful countryside.

Right: Annie Pit winder men: Bunty Smith (banksman), Jack Souter (winder engine man), Mick Curry (shaftsman) and Andrew Scott (engine winder man). Jack Thompson took this photo. He worked there until the colliery closed in 1949.

14

Burnhope Collieries By Jim Bradley

These sketches are by local artist Jim Bradley. Jim was head of art at Stanley School of Technology, and was for some time responsible for art throughout the County Education system. Everyone who knows the Burnhope collieries say his sketches on them are almost identical, with incredible detail. I am proud to have a print of one of them hanging in my home. For many years, the four sketches he did, hung in the Doctor's surgery at Burnhope.

Above and below: Burnhope Colliery by Jim Bradley.

Burnhope Fortune Pit by Jim Bradley.

Office Row, Burnhope Colliery by Jim Bradley.

Burnopfield Colliery
The Hobson

This colliery first opened in 1742. However, before that the monks used to mine bell pits. There is photographic evidence of these primitive mining methods in recent years when they excavated the area for new housing. The first of the owners in the later, traditional form of mining were Messrs Bowes, Hutt, Wood & Charles M. Palmer in the 1850s. They were succeeded in the 1860s by the Marley Hill Coal Co. It then reverted to John Bowes & Partners in the 1880s until the National Coal Board in 1947. The colliery closed in August 1968. The highest number employed was in 1960 with 669 men above and below ground.

The Hobson Colliery winder house.

Some of the seams worked were: Busty Bank, Main, Brass Thill, Busty, Hutton, Main Coal, Brockwell, Five Quarter, Shield Row and Section.

Two of the many of those killed included Austin O'Rourke, aged 18 in 1926, caught by the cage and dragged into the shaft. William Locket, aged 41 in 1883, crushed by cage at shaft top.

Like most collieries there were a selection of miners' houses near to the pit head. There was also a Methodist Chapel, and a school at nearby Pickering Nook.

After closure, the colliery buildings were used to form an industrial estate, which still exists today in 2009.

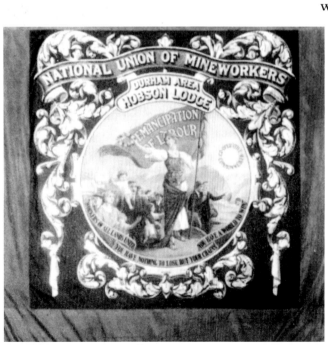

Hobson Colliery Lodge Banner.

Hobson Colliery official.

Above:
The man
on the
right is
Syd Yard
of the
Hobson.

Right:
Two
photos of
Hobson
Colliery at
the start of
demolition
in 1968 by
Ernie
Yard.

Byermoor Colliery

Byermoor Colliery was opened by Marley Hill Coal Co in 1860. It was later owned by John Bowes & Partners and finally the NCB. It closed in February 1968. The highest number of employees was in 1914 with 459 men and boys. The seams worked were the Brockwell, Busty, Three Quarter and Tilley.

A boy aged just 12 named George Knott was killed in 1875 when he was run over by a coal tub. At the other end of the age spectrum, 66 year old W. Taylor was killed in 1948 by a runaway set.

Many men from the Stanley area worked at Byermoor.

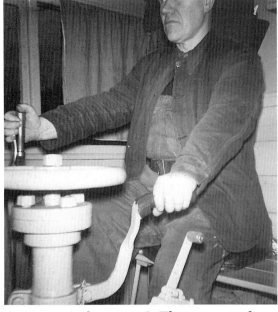

Engine winder man J. Thompson who was a keen photographer of colliery images.

Byermoor Upcast Shaft

Byermoor Colliery First Aid Team. Back row: C. Metcalfe, W. Mackie, E. Gibson, J. Bainbridge and A. Robson. Front row: Major Nicholson, Sir Myers Wayman and C. Mills.

Ronnie Richardson (safety officer), Fred Watson and Bob Gray (joiners), Jack Nelson (blacksmith) and George Elliott (blacksmith) up the ladder.

Causey Arch

Building work began on the Causey Arch around 1725. This huge civil engineering project was funded by a group known as 'The Grand Allies' and was made up of Colonel Liddell, the Hon Charles Montague, Sir John Clavering, George Bowes, Thomas Brumell, and others. These were a group of coal and land owners, and it was in their interest to take control of getting the coal from their mines down to the Tyne without being held to ransom over charges by rival coal owners.

Ralph Wood, a local stonemason and engineer was given the contract and there are conflicting accounts as to what happened during the construction. One theory is that Wood constructed a wooden arch which collapsed. After then building the stone structure, he is supposed to have thrown himself to his death from the arch, fearful of a repeat of the wooden arch. There is no evidence if this actually occurred or not. Another account says the wooden construction was only the template for the stonework, and that it was the wooden framework that collapsed, leaving the stonework untouched.

In my book *Looking Back At Stanley* is a cost account of building the Causey Arch, and it shows that a man named Hugh Boag either joined Wood, or took over the construction of the arch from July 1726 and worked on it until completion. It gives no reason why. Maybe they worked together. The total cost of the arch was £2,141 15s 1d. This costing was for the arch only and not the surrounding work.

The bridge has a span of 105 feet, just over 22 feet wide and 80 feet high. There was a double timber track for the wagons to cross. The wooden chauldrons were pulled by horses and approx. 930 wagons crossed the bridge in each direction every day, some 50 feet apart. The distance from Tanfield Moor to the Teams Staithes was approx seven miles although with the various branches to other collieries connected to it, this length was much longer. The bridge was originally named Dawson Bridge because the land was owned by Thomas Dawson, who is believed to have had a drift mine near the site.

The Causey Arch has been restored by the local authority in recent years and has thousands of visitors every year to the added picnic area, and of course, its links with Tanfield Railway.

This sketch gives a good insight as to how it was when working all those years ago.

Three modern photographs showing
Causey Arch and its surroundings.

Craghead Collieries

William Hedley came to Craghead in 1839 and proceeded to sink the William Pit. He was born at Newburn in 1779. He was viewer at Walbottle and then later also at Wylam Colliery. He discovered and demonstrated to people like Stephenson the efficiency of traction by smooth wheel on smooth wheel. He tried his first engine in 1813 built by Thomas Salter, but it was short of steam power. In May 1913, his second engine, the Puffing Billy, was fitted with a return boiler which proved successful. He built the Wylam Dilly at the same time and these two engines ran between Wylam and the Tyne Staithes. William Hedley died at his home in Burnopside in 1843.

Right: Pictured at the Wylam Dilly at Craghead Colliery are: William Hedley Jnr, and one of his brothers. On the loco extreme right is Mr J. Robson. He was one of several generations of loco drivers at Craghead Colliery.

The Hedleys brought the Wylam Dilly to Craghead Colliery in 1862, where it stayed until 1879 when it was sent to Edinburgh Chambers Museum. The Hedleys went on to sink the George in 1854, the Oswald in 1878, the Edward in 1909 and Thomas. While sinking the William Pit in 1839, they found good quality clay and they opened a brickworks at Craghead and these bricks were used to build the early houses at Craghead and South Moor.

Above: Craghead in the 1960s.

Craghead Colliery closed in 1968. Some of the men transferred down to the Nottingham area, while others made redundant obtained work locally. Some of the older ones retired. For a while, it looked like the village might die with Category 'D' threatening to demolish the houses and disburse the community.

They did not reckon on the power of the people of Craghead. They stayed together, formed a committee to bring the village up to date, and with the addition of new houses and a general improvement, Craghead is now a desirable place to live. It boasts a golf course, two public houses, two working men's clubs, a post office, village hall and health centre. This plus an industrial estate, plus of course the school.

Left: Jack Forster, the former boxer, knocker up at Bloemfontein.

The Locomotives of Craghead Colliery

William Hedley introduced the Wylam Dilly at Craghead in 1862, where it remained until 1879. The second engine, built by Dunston Engineering Works at Gatehead came in 1879. Burnopside (pictured) was probably a prototype built by Black Hawthorne for the Newcastle Exhibition in 1887, and named Victoria. It was bought by William Hedley Jnr that year but demanded the name be changed to Burnopside before delivery. The early loco colours were light and dark green lined with black and red. This lasted until Nationalisation in 1947 when the colours changed to blue with numbers instead of names. Burnopside was scrapped in 1957.

Holmside No 2 was built in 1901 by Chapman-Ferneux and worked between Craghead Colliery and the Morrison. It was later numbered No 35 and was scrapped in 1962. Holmside Engines Nos 3 & 4 were saddle tank engines built by Hawthorne Leslie (year unknown). After Nationalisation they became engines 36 and 37. Holmside No 3 was stationed at Craghead and stayed there until the colliery closed.

NCB Locomotive No 80 was built by Robert Stephenson & Hawthorne and came to Craghead in 1949 and worked there until 1967. It was then transferred to Handon Hold Engine Sheds along with Engine No 36. Road haulage took over from then at Craghead Colliery.

The driver of Burnopside as shown was W.G. Robson, one of several generations of Robsons who worked on the locos at Craghead Colliery. (Information from the late Jim Robson.)

The locomotive Burnopside.

Underground at Craghead.

Craghead Colliery Silver Prize Band.

Craghead Lodge, band and banner at Durham.

Craghead Lodge carrying their banner into Durham Cathedral on Miners' Gala Day for a blessing in 1956.

Craghead Colliery Lodge, band and banner at Craghead after being awarded the NCB Production Banner.

Charlie Pit
New Shield Row Colliery

This colliery was named the New Shield Row Colliery, then Quaking Houses Colliery and finally the Charlie Pit. It was actually situated between Sandhole and Quaking Houses to the west of South Moor. It was originally on the site called Quaking House Farm near to Quaking House Hill. There were some cottages nearby named Quakers Cottages, after the Quakers who lived there.

The colliery was sunk in 1845 by William Bell & Ptnrs. The first coals were sent away in 1846 when the Pea Pit at Oxhill closed. The large Waddle fan was installed in 1893. This was replaced with a high speed Sirocco Fan in 1907.

Due to the abundance of clay in the area, the colliery opened its own brickworks which replaced Craghead Colliery Brickworks. The largest quarry was to the rear of the Upper Standards School. This quarry closed in 1948 and was levelled. The last of the chimneys was demolished in 1975 when children from Greenland School were allowed to watch the chimney fall. There was a coal depot nearby.

The Charlie Pit. Note the large Waddle Fan on the right.

Above: The Charlie Pit Brickworks. Bricks from here were used to build many of the local houses and even Holmside & South Moor Welfare Fund Hospital. Quite often, an aerial tubway was used to transport the bricks. As a pupil at Annfield Plain Secondary School, we used to have to run around the brickworks two times as part of our cross country. Some of those who smoked never ran around and just waited for the rest to start the journey back up the hill to the Upper Standards School, and then joined in again.

Charlie Pit workers and the steam traction engine at the colliery.

The Charlie Pit after closure.

Dipton Delight Pit

The Delight Pit was owned by the Marley Hill Coal Co Ltd and was originally named the Dipton Colliery, and worked by Messrs. John Bowes, William Hutt, Nicholas Wood, and Charles Mark Palmer. The first of the Delight pits was sunk in 1842. A second shaft was sunk at the Delight in 1853. In 1855, William Elliott aged 11 fell down the shaft and was killed. The Surtees was sunk in 1883. Seams worked at the Delight Pit were: Shield Row, Five Quarter, Brass Thill, Hutton, Main Coal and Busty. In 1879, there was great disruption to the colliery with arson and structural damage due to strikes. The highest number of employees seems to have been in 1940 with 850 workers. There was a coke and gas works adjoining the colliery. The Delight closed in 1940.

For some reason, the pit ponies were above ground at the Delight Pit and there was pony racing. Whether this was an annual event, I'm not sure. The photo was taken in the 1920s. Note the gas works behind.

Left: This newer photo of the Delight Pit shows the colliery winding gear, engine house and a large supply of timber ready to go underground. We were lucky in our region as there was a good supply of timber drawn from the local woods.

Right: Mr Bolam, a Dipton miner pictured with a pit pony near his home. I'm not sure why.

Dipton, like most of our villages had a good mixture of churches, with Church of England, Roman Catholic, Primitive, Wesleyan and United Free Methodists, and of course, the Salvation Army.

They were equally well served with pubs with the Red Lion, Sportsman Arms, The Fox, The Bute and many others. They also had, and still have, Dipton Working Men's Club.

This was the last club in our area to allow women into the club. There were, and still are, the Scouts, Guides, Cubs and Brownies. Dipton has always been well renowned for its sporting activities, There was a Co-operative store, butchers, bakers, chemists and all the shops needed. The village was self sufficient in almost every way.

Left: After closure in 1940. The end of an era.

East Castle

East Castle Colliery was sunk around 1860 by Bainbridge, Kissop & Co. It was then owned by East Castle Coal Co and East Pontop Coal Co. It closed for a while, but reopened in 1868. The highest number of employees seems to have been in 1896 with 174 staff. The seams then worked were the Brass Thill, Five Quarter, and Shield Row. The annual output was 100,000 tons of coal. They also had 74 coke ovens. Nearby were the lime kilns of the Stanhope & Tyne Railway. These kilns had a castle shaped roof, hence the name of the village, East Castle. In 1874, James Jackson aged 47, a deputy, was asphyxiated by carbonic acid gas. In 1882, Henry Stobbs aged 66, a furnaceman was crushed to his death by tubs on an engine plane.

Right: East Castle Village.

East Pontop Colliery

East Pontop Colliery was opened by Bainbridge Kissop & Co around 1880 and later owned by East Castle Coal Co and East Pontop Coal Co. There were 471 employed in 1914. It closed in 1930. The seams worked were: the Crow Coal, Brass Thill, Five Quarter, Hutton and Shield Row. In 1875, John Dawson aged 25, a furnaceman fell to his death down the air shaft. In 1920, Ralph Calvert Hodge, aged 23 was killed by a fall of stone only five minutes after starting work.

A present day photograph of the former Stanhope & Tyne lime kilns at East Castle.

East Stanley Colliery (Jackie's Pit)

East Stanley Colliery (Jackie's Pit) was situated between No Place and East Stanley and could be reached under the bridge at No Place. Sinking began in 1863 by Joicey and the shaft bottom was reached in 1864. Joicey sold the colliery in 1930 to the Derwent Coal Co. It finally closed in 1937. It is believed that at one time, there was a Methodist Chapel on this site.

Left and below:
Two photographs from Beamish Museum's Archive of the demolition of East Stanley Colliery (Jackie's Pit) after closure.

East Tanfield Colliery and Causey Mill Drift

East Tanfield Colliery was opened by James Joicey in 1844. Other owners were East Tanfield Colliery Co, South Derwent Coal Co and the NCB. It was originally known as the Engine Pit. In 1940 there were 890 employees. They worked the Brockwell, Busty Bank, Hutton, Main Beaumont, Five Quarter, Three Quarter and Tilley seams.

One of two men who died was Robert Hindhaugh Scurr, in 1934, aged 14. While working on the screens he got his clothes entangled in the machine and was drawn into the mechanism. He died a few hours later of multiple injuries. Robert Baker was killed in 1908, aged 16, he was a driver and was thrown from tubs and crushed.

There was a drift mine to East Tanfield and output from here helped in the award of the Production Banner. My father said the two shafts were very close to each other, only separated by brickwork.

The Causey Mill Drift could be reached by road via the Old Causey Road. It opened in 1949 and closed in 1955. They worked the Hutton and Low Main seams. At times, they were so close to the surface, that once a cow fell into the workings and had to be slaughtered.

Above: East Tanfield Colliery.

Right: An early photo of East Tanfield miners.

Three engineering staff at East Tanfield: Nelson, Brown and Manistre.

East Tanfield engineering staff, electricians, blacksmiths etc, including: Jack Hockaday, F. Ions, J. Smith, W. Houston, G. Robinson, G. Harrison, D. Biggs, W. Rowell, ? Grey and E. Stewart.

The Last Shift at East Tanfield, including: E. Piper, T. Cooper, Pop McGuire, C. Sloane, N. Whiteford and B. Johnson.

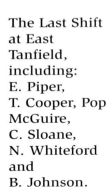

A selection of wooden tools were found at East Tanfield and these were handed over to Stanley Urban District Council. Their whereabouts are now unknown.

East Tanfield Colliery Lodge Banner and Officials. Included are: ? Pearson, T. Jackson, J. Clarkson, W. Hair, E. Sheavils, J. Bevan, J. Coulson, S. Walker, J. McKendrick, T. Anderson and others.

Men on the last shift at the colliery.

Handon Hold Colliery

Over the years, the title of this pit was spelt several different ways – eg. Handenhold, Handen Hold and Hand In Hold.

This colliery opened in 1860 and closed in March 1968. As far as I can gather it was known as Six Feet Staple. The known owners were Sir James Joicey, then Lambton, Hetton and Joicey and finally the NCB. The highest number of miners employed was in 1921 with 768 men. They worked the Hutton, Low Main, Beaumont, Five Quarter, Busty, Maudlin, Shield Row, Brockwell, Tilley and Low Brockwell over the years it was open. The colliery was situated at West Pelton.

Two unusual deaths occurred; firstly Nicholson Johnson Robinson, aged 19 in 1908, a driver, was kicked in the head by a pony. Secondly, Thomas Armstrong, aged 14, died in 1899. He was a landing boy, and a set of tubs left the rails and ran into a full set behind which the boy was standing.

Left: In the boilerhouse at Handon Hold Colliery. On the right is Bob Lawson.

Pontop Colliery

Pontop Colliery opened the Cresswell Colliery in the 1760s followed by Hare Law Pit in 1839 and the South Pit also in 1839. The owners were Lady Windsor and John Simpson, John Bowes & Co, the Marley Hill Coal Co and John Bowes & Ptnrs. It must have been a fairly large colliery, as in 1914, they employed 545 men. They worked the Brass Thill, Five Quarter, Hutton and Main Coal seams.

In 1890, John Pearson, aged 13, a driver, was killed on an engine plane on leaving a refuge hole too soon. In 1919, A. Stewart, aged 15, a pony driver was killed when his hand was caught fast between a tub and a prop. In 1901, another 13 year old, Jonathan Tweddle was killed as the result of sitting on some tubs just when the pony stumbled, knocking out some timbers, and caused a roof fall.

Do you have any information on this colliery?

There were many collieries in this area of Pontop, Hare Law, Greencroft and Kyo. Much of the information is a little confusing with some of the pits having the same names. There were actually 33 pits in this district alone. For this reason, I have stuck to the main known collieries and owners. If you have any information on Hare Law Pit, please let me know and I will add it at a later date. I have some time sheets somewhere which show the Rodham family working at Hare Law. It was father and son. The son was the great-grandfather of Hillary Rodham Clinton, wife of Bill Clinton, former President of the United States of America. Her great-grandfather moved from Hare Law Pit to Oxhill before emigrating to America.

High Stables Colliery
South Medomsley

A group of Teesside business men purchased an area of land at the west of Dipton in 1863. Test boring resulted in finding twelve seams of coal, and a shaft was sunk. A second shaft, the Mary, was sunk in Pont Valley in 1867. The colliery had a fatal accident in 1934 when a gas explosion in the Busty Seam killed three men. Owned by Dickinson & Surtees, the colliery was taken over by the South Medomsley Coal Co in 1902 when the previous owners went bankrupt. This prevented the closure of the colliery. The NCB took over in 1947, and in 1963, it became part of the Eden Colliery after joining up underground. The colliery closed in 1980.

Above: Billy Marrs at the blacksmiths.

Left: Pit cages at High Stables.

N. Oyston, N. Thornton and J. Allaker.

B. Temple, H. Chipchase, G. Ramsey, J. Allaker, C. Sayers and F. Rochester outside the lamp cabin.

Disaster at High Stables, 29th March 1934
A gas explosion killed 3 men

Those killed: Joseph Merrington, Luke Newton, George Nicholson. They were all buried at East Castle Cemetery.

The two survivors who were: David Gregory and Christopher Young.

The explosion occurred at approx 2.30 pm on 29th March 1934 in the Top Busty Seam of South Medomsley Colliery. Inflammable gas was, until then, unknown in any of the seams being worked in this area, and was therefore worked with naked lights. The explosion was confined to the East Landing South Flat. The seam being worked was the top Busty, and the coal was three feet thick with a sandstone roof.

At the time of the explosion, there were five miners in this district. David Gregory (deputy), Joseph Merrington, George Nicholson, Christopher Young (coal hewers) and Luke Newton (pony putter).

On 28th March, the roof supports were withdrawn from a complete lift, and the roof fell to a smooth bedding plane. At about 10.00 am on the following day Christopher Young commenced a new lift which happened to be the last off the same pillars. About 2.30 pm, he was sticking his candle holder into the top of the prop nearest to the face on the goaf side, when the flame of the candle ignited firedamp. Young threw himself to the ground for a moment or two, then, after covering his mouth and his nose with his shirt, commenced to make his way outbye. He did this in the dark, his two candles having been extinguished. On the 'going bord' he was knocked down by the blast of air, but recovered himself and continued outbye before collapsing finally near a body, apparently lifeless. He thought, by the build, it was that of George Nicholson.

The deputy, George Gregory was at the face of the outbye headings when he heard the loud report, and saw flames coming through the bord just outbye. He was knocked down, but hearing the putter, Luke Newton, shouting from the next holding inbye, he tried to crawl outbye along the headways. However, he soon collapsed and became unconscious. Young and George were the only two who survived.

Rolleywayman Alexander Stewart who, with a landing lad, was about 170 yards from the face by the most direct route when he was knocked to the ground by the blast which extinguished their lights. Stewart and the lad went outbye some distance in the dark before relighting their lights. They continued until they reached a phone. Overman Thomas Bolam answered the phone some two miles away and made his way toward Stewart. He also phoned the manager at the surface informing him of the events.

On arrival at the scene, Bolam withdrew the miners from the bottom Busty. By then, the manager, Mr Davidson had arrived and he sent Stewart to phone for the Rescue Brigade. Davidson and Bolam attempted to enter the explosion area. At the flat they found a good deal of smoke becoming thicker inbye. They found Nicholson and Merrington, both apparently dead. Further inbye, they found Gregory alive, but unconscious. They dragged him outbye for some distance, but had to cease as the manager was overcome with the poison fumes. In the meantime, Stewart returned to the landing, and he and Bolam made a further rescue attempt taking a tram with them. On the way inbye, they were joined by a deputy named

High Stables Colliery.

Crossley. When they reached Gregory, they found Young there also, both unconscious. They were placed on the tram and brought outbye, and transferred onto a haulage set accompanied by Bolam. The Elswick Rescue Brigade arrive by 4.12 pm. The district affected was some 2,000 yards from the shaft. The first body was brought back to the landing in an hour from the time of the arrival of the Brigade.

The explosion originated at the flame of Young's candle, and travelled through the goaf to Nicholson's and Merrington's places, then through the middle and outbye headings, to the main parallel headways.

Coal dust played little or no part in the explosion until the main headways was reached when, possibly raised by the gas explosion sweeping through the goaf, it was ignited in quantity sufficient to propagate flame to the flat. A total distance of about 300 yards along the path travelling from the point of origin. There was no evidence of force other than a few brattice sheets blown down, due mainly to the relief afforded by the different paths available. The roof cavity in the goaf to the left of Young's place of work, must have been full of firedamp by the time of the explosion, and was probably full when Deputy Gregory examined the face of Young's working place half an hour before. Gregory did not examine for firedamp in this cavity as it was outside the limits of the working place and, in his opinion, it would have been definitely dangerous to do so. In this opinion, he was supported by all the other witnesses.

The amount of ventilation provided was adequate, but it was considered just possible that had an additional brattice sheet been placed, sufficient air would have pulled along the goaf edge to prevent the accumulation in the cavity, of firedamp in explosive concentration. As a result of this explosion, safety lamps were introduced into all three working seams. Carnoustie Hero Fund Trust Certificates and Awards were received for their bravery by Davidson, Bolam, Stewart and Crossley.

From an article in *The Times* on 31st March, I give a summary of what was written.

Three miners were killed and two others gassed in an explosion at South Medomsley Colliery, Dipton, North West Durham. The explosion took place in the High Busty Seam, about 500 yards below the surface, and about one mile from the shaft bottom. The manager, Mr Davison, who was one of the first on the scene was carried out on a stretcher suffering from afterdamp. The three dead were described as, Joseph Merrington, aged 37, hewer, married with one child. George Nicholson, aged 26, hewer, married with two children and Luke Newton, aged 21, a putter, unmarried. The two recovering from the gas are Christopher Young and David Gregory. One pit pony was killed. All the men came from Dipton. Christopher Young gave an account of his experience. He saw a flash of flame coming from the coal face and realised there was going to be an explosion. The roof held, and he began to crawl out on all fours with his shirt stuffed in his mouth. He heard the cries of Nicholson in the dark, and crawled past him, but realised that it was too late to help him. There had been twelve men in the seam, but only five remained at the time of the explosion, and they were about to leave the coal face for the shaft bottom.

High Stables Colliery.

37

Lord James Joicey

James Joicey was probably the most successful of the coal owners in the north of England. He was born in Kip Hill in a red tiled house just below the Ball Alley (Shield Row Hotel) in 1846. His father was George Joicey. He was a partner in the Newcastle firm of engineers, J & G Joicey. The first colliery acquired by the Joicey family was South Tanfield at Oxhill in 1848. George died when James was only nine years old. When James was 17 years old, he began working in his uncle's Newcastle office. Within one month of starting work there, his uncle, James Joicey, died. At that time, Edward and John Joicey were the partners. Young James became a partner in 1867 and soon took control of the day to day running of the company.

At sometime after this, the Joicey's purchased the Lambton Group of companies from the Earl of Durham. The success during the next year made James Joicey £1,000,000 profit which was a phenomenal amount at that time and he had all the country talking of him. That in such a short time, he had collieries that were between them producing annually an output of 6 million tons. He was the leading mine owner when he entered Parliament as MP for Chester-le-Street in 1885, a position he held until 1906. Also in 1885, he started the Newcastle newspaper *The Daily Leader*.

Joicey became a Baronet in 1895 and Baron Joicey of Chester-le-Street and Ford in 1905. He was also Chairman of the Tanfield Steamship Co Ltd, Chairman of the Northern Coal Co Ltd of Australia, chairman of the Albyn Steamship Co, Sunderland and a director of LNER. Though regarded as one of the most successful men in the business world, he was described in his private life as being courteous, kindly and a simple man. He never lost sight of where he came from and supposedly remained unspoilt by his success, but justly proud of the career he had carved out with his own hands. The Joicey Co built hundreds of houses in the Stanley area including Joicey Square, Joicey Terrace at Oxhill and Joicey Terrace at Tanfield Lea.

Among the pits owned by Lord Joicey were: South Tanfield, Beamish Air Pit, Beamish No 2, Beamish Mary, East Stanley, East Tanfield, Handon Hold, Tanfield Moor, Tanfield Lea, and others.

Almost up to his death, he controlled his company which he kept in the hands of his family. He was President of the Newcastle & Gateshead Chamber of Commerce for many years.

He was married twice. His first wife, Elizabeth Arny died in 1881. His second wife, Margaret Smyles, died in 1911. Lord Joicey died in his residence, Ford Castle, Northumberland on 21st November 1936 aged 90. His heir was the Hon. James Arthur Joicey, his eldest son, although he and his brother Sydney became joint managing directors of the company.

Fox Pit or Machine Pit

The Fox Pit was just to the east of the Pea Farm and was worked during the 18th century though I have no dates for opening or closing. This was a corfe pit worked by a horse drawn gin. It was of the whim gin type with a wooden drum with levers underneath, attached to a pair of horses. This was one of the oldest pits in our region. They used eight horses a shift with two horses at a time for two hours. The corfes were no more than circular baskets made of hazel rods and could carry approx 3 cwts. As each corfe was lowered empty, a full one was hauled to the surface. There were no rails or guard around the top of the circular shaft, and during the 18th century, many men fell to their deaths, but they did not keep a record of their names. The coal was taken by black wagons on wooden railway chauldrons, each carried 53 cwts to Kip Hill from where it went along to Tanfield Causey Waggonway and on down to the River Tyne, or via Beamish to Fatfield and the River Wear. The colliery's name was later changed to the Machine Pit.

Kibblesworth Colliery

This colliery opened in 1842 and closed in October 1974. There were two pits, the Glamis and the Robert. Although Kibblesworth was not in our area, my father went to work there when East Tanfield was closed. Even though he had suffered terrible injuries including broken bones in his spine, he was given what was described as 'light work' pushing and pulling the tubs into the shaft cage. After a lifetime in the pits, there was no one there on his last shift to thank him for all those years underground. Shame on them.

There were five men killed due to boiler explosions: Joseph Askew in 1876; John Bewley, engineer, in 1855; Edmund Cuft, fireman, in 1856; Joseph Hindmarsh, aged 41, in 1876; Thomas Leadbitter, fireman, in 1856.

It appears there were three explosions with two men dying in each of two of the three explosions.

Kibblesworth Colliery. 3630

Lintz Colliery – Anna and Billy Pits

The Anna Pit opened in 1855 and closed in 1929. The owners were McLean & Prior, John Shield Esq and South Garesfield Colliery Co. There was also the Billy Pit a short distance away. In 1921, they employed 458.

Lintz Anna Pit.

Lintz Billy Pit.

Louisa Colliery, Stanley

This colliery was situated at the top of Stanley Front Street. Some of the older maps show it as South Moor Colliery No 1. That is because it was owned by the South Moor Coal Co. It opened in 1863 and closed in 1964. Apart from the Louisa coal, it also received coal over the years from the Hedley and William Pits at South Moor, Shield Row Drift, Oakey's Pit and others, some of these from underground and others by rail. In 1921, there were 2,427 men employed at the Louisa New and Old Pits. Certain areas of this colliery could be reached by three shafts, the Louisa, the William Pit at Old South Moor and the Morrison North Pit. There was a serious explosion in the Fourth North District in 1947 killing 22 men.

There were two major collieries in the town centre of Stanley, the Louisa and the West Stanley Colliery. However, there were many other smaller pits.

Right: A view along Louisa Terrace toward the Louisa Colliery.

Left: The gate way at the Louisa Colliery with NCB lorries waiting to be loaded with the miner's fuel allowance. Coal was delivered to the homes of the miners monthly. As a boy, I put in many a load of coal at home, while my father was at work. This site is now Asda Super Store.

The rail crossing from Louisa Colliery. This once went down to Oakey's Pit which closed in the 1930s. It also went over to the Louisa cokeworks. Now the site of the Louisa Sports Centre.

The Louisa Coke Works. When they were building Netto, a section of road on the east side of the Louisa Sports Centre was excavated and a short stretch of narrow gauge railway was exposed. I rushed home for my camera, but they had dug it up before I got back to the site.

Louisa staff including: Les Clennel, Rob McGregor, Bill Woolcock, Tom Kilkenny, George Sharp.

The Louisa First Aid and Rescue Team.

Rail lines into the Louisa Colliery. An incline waggonway hauled coals up from the Hedley and William Pits at Old South Moor. Coal was then sent by rail down the Pontop to South Shields Railway via Stanley Hilltop.

T. Kilkenney at his home in Louisa Terrace. He was an engine winder man at the Louisa.

Marley Hill Colliery

This colliery was opened in 1841 by John Bowes & Ptnrs which included, Bowes, Hutt, Wood and Charles Palmer. The Queen Mother was a Bowes Lyon and the family owns a large area of land in this district. The colliery was taken over on Vesting Day in January 1947 by the NCB. The colliery closed in March 1983. Many of the miners at this colliery came from the Stanley area. The highest number of men employed here was in 1975 with 948 men.

In 1840 it was known as the Lodge Pit. The seams worked were: Brockwell, Busty, Main Coal, Hutton, Brass Thill, Tilley, Low Main, Yard and Harvey. There was an unsolved robbery at Marley Hill Colliery in the 1950s when someone stole the wages from the colliery office. Many say they knew who did this, but no one was ever arrested.

The loco sheds of this colliery are still in existence (2009) and are part of the Tanfield Railway. They are supposedly the oldest existing railway sheds in the world. There was a coke and gas works at Marley Hill. The miners' housing was very close to the pit head, as was the Methodist Church.

Right: Note how close the Methodist Church is to the colliery.

Marley Hill Colliery.

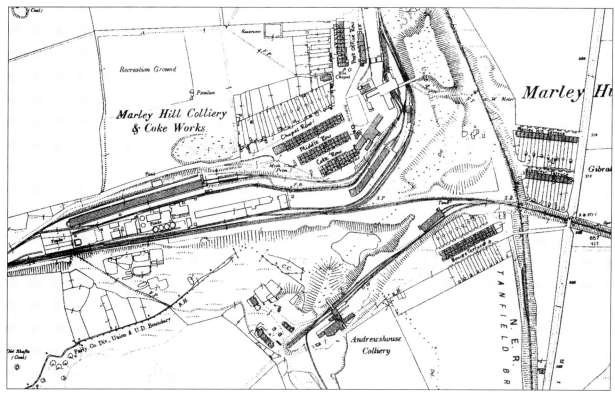

A map of Marley Hill Colliery. Note some of the houses and how close they actually were – Chapel Row, Middle Row, Coke Row and others. There was also a recreation field next to the Cokeworks. Most, but not all of these houses had large gardens.

This photograph was taken by Ron Hindhaugh of Tanfield Village.

Marley Hill Cokeworks.

Four Marley Hill miners on their day off.

Chapel Row. The small building on the left was the corner shop. The chapel was at the far end of the street. These houses and Coke Row were demolished in the 1930s. Middle Row survived to approx 1960.

Left: This street was named 'The Hole'. An earth bank behind these houses slipped during a rainy period and covered one of the middle houses. No one was hurt.

Right: A typical house in Chapel Row. Much of this information is from the excellent Tanfield Railway Book available at the Railway Shop.

Blackburn Fell Drift Mine

This drift mine was opposite Marley Hill Colliery on the Andrews House to Sunniside Road. It was opened by John Bowes & Ptnrs in July 1937. It closed in February 1979. Over two hundred men worked here. They worked the Brass Thill and Yard.

Underground at Blackburn Fell Drift.

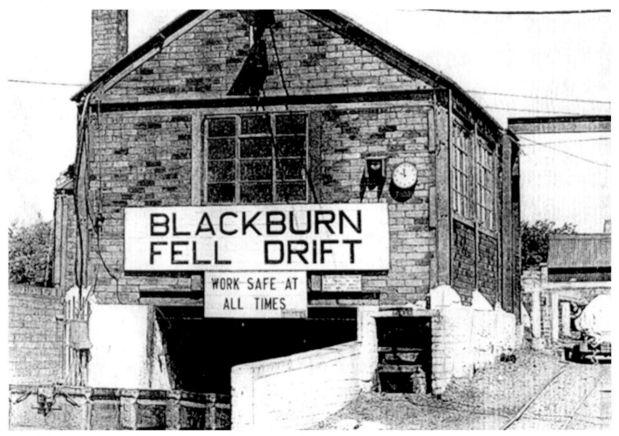

Blackburn Fell Drift, part of Marley Hill Colliery.

Miners' Sunday

Miners' Sunday was introduced in Stanley in 1953 at the suggestion of Methodist Minister P. Davison. The first of these services was held in Stanley Wesleyan Methodist Church on Front Street. Even though this church could seat 1,000, such was the huge number who attended, it was decided to hold all future meetings outdoors. This was justified when over 2,000 people attended the meeting at the King's Head Field as can be seen in the photo below. There was a parade of the colliery lodges through Stanley including bands and banners plus the band of the Salvation Army. Some of those in attendance were: South Moor Nos 1 & 2, Morrison Busty, Beamish, Craghead, Tanfield Lea, East Tanfield, Burnhope, and Crookhall. Sam Watson, Secretary of the Durham Miner's Association, was also there. The sermon was given by Lord Lawson of Beamish and the service was read by local coal miner, I. Edwards of South Moor. The bands were conducted by Norman Nattrass and the mass choirs were led by Norman Williams. In the evening, there were several local church services for the bereaved and injured.

Holding a service on the King's Head Field.

Miners' Sunday Parade at the lower end of Front Street.

Morrison Collieries
North and Busty

The Morrison North and South Pits were sunk in 1868, and opened in 1869. Shortly after this they erected a double battery of Beehive Coke Ovens. The pit was idle from 1876 to 1891. The major owners were, Morrison, Bell, Hunter & Ptnrs and the South Moor Coal Co Ltd, until it was Nationalised in January 1947. The seams worked were the Morrison, Five Quarter, Hutton, Low Main, Main and Maudlin. In 1921, this colliery is listed as having 1,946 employed, but I am not sure if these figures include other collieries in the South Moor Coal Co. This section of the colliery closed in 1948. The Morrison Busty was sunk in 1923 with shafts East and West, but strangely did not open until 1927. Owners are listed as the Holmside & South Moor Coal Co and the NCB. This colliery closed in October 1973.

Buildings from both of these collieries are still in use as industrial estates and for many years the base for Derwentside District Council.

In 1947, there was a serious event at the 4th North District. This section underground was served from three shafts: South Moor William Pit; the Louisa Pit at Stanley; and the Morrison North Pit. Because of a problem with differing conditions concerning gas and non gassy working conditions, it was decided to bring all men working the 4th North under one Lodge, and declare the area as 'Gassy' to be worked with safety lamp.

An explosion occurred in 1947 causing the death of 22 miners.

A view of the old chimney of the North Pit with St Aidan's Church in the distance, taken in the 1920s.

Left: The Morrison North Pit.

Above & right:
Two photos in
the 1920s of
Morrison
North & South
Pits.

Morrison North and South Pits in the 1890s.

Morrison North Pit in later years.

Diesel locomotive underground at Morrison. Do you know the name of the people in the photo?

Morrison Colliery Band at Annfield Plain. The MP Jimmy Glanville is at the extreme right of photo.

Two views of the Morrison Busty Colliery.

The Morrison Busty under construction in 1923.

A postcard view of the Morrison Busty Colliery produced by the Gateshead photographer Robert Johnston.

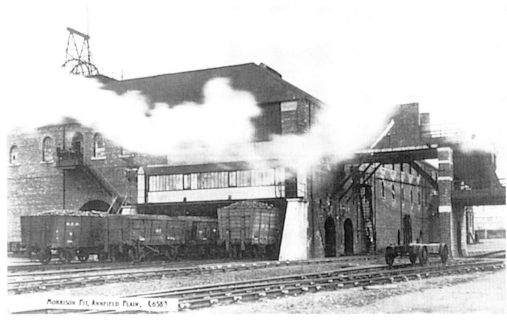

Morrison Busty Collieries East and West. The East Pit heapstead is nearest to the camera. The building on the right is part of the dust collector taking unburnt coal dust from chimney flue.

Morrison Busty Fan House under construction in 1923.

A group of electricians at the Morrison Busty Colliery during the 1940s, pictured in the doorway of the Fan House. They are, left to right, standing: Albert Wilkinson, Assistant Electrical Engineer, Norman Dixon, Electrical Engineer, Vender Hunter. Sitting: Bill Wilson (just out of the Navy), Len Kay, John Hubble (Bevin Boy), Jack Harrison, Jeff Robertson (just out of the Air Force.

Morrison electricians outside the Morrison West Pit sinking engine house emergency winder. They are, left to right: standing: Arthur Bragan, Albert Aitchieson, George Muncaster, Alan Ambler. Crouching: Jack Nicholson, Jack McHugh.

A group of electricians at the Morrison Busty Colliery in the 1940s. Left to right, standing: Jeff Robertson, Bill Wilson, George Muncaster, Norman Dixon, Bill ?, Charlie Nixon, Albert Wilkinson. Crouching: Vender Hunter, Len Kay, Johnny Hubble (Bevin Boy).

This photo at the Morrison Busty Colliery was taken just after Vesting Day in January 1947. Vesting Day was the day the Government took over many of the collieries in the country under Nationalisation. Those who worked at well run private coal mines thought it was a good thing, while others thought there was no change in the bad habits of the former private ownership, with only a change of name. Pictured at the Morrison are Vender Henderson and Len Kay. Photo by George Muncaster.

Above: The Morrison Busty Lodge Banner.

Right: The Miners' Institute at New Kyo. Inside were a dance hall, meeting rooms, a library, snooker room and swimming pool. This was situated behind Sycamore Terrace.

Above & below: Trainees at former Bevin Boy huts at New Kyo.

Louisa Morrison Colliery Disaster
22nd-23rd August 1947

In this underground explosion at the 4th North District, 22 miners lost their lives due to the illegal striking of a Lucifer match. The names of those who died are as follows:

Thomas William Appleby
Alfred Bailey
Thomas Bell (1)
Thomas Bell (2)
Robert William Birtle
Reginald Leslie Brown
Joseph Chapman
John Estell
Norman Fenwick
John Grimley
Joseph Hodgson

Francis Eric Martin (Bevin Boy)
Thomas McKever
Gerald Raymond Moore (Bevin Boy)
William Reed
Walter Rowe
John Robert Rowland
William Rutherford
Colin Simpson
Harry Talbot
Edward Westgarth
Clement Minto

The two survivors were W.H. Johnson and J. Kilgallon.

The official name of the disaster was the Louisa Colliery Disaster, however, it is known locally as the Morrison Disaster. The explosion occurred in the 4th North District. This could be reached by the Louisa, South Moor William Pit and the Morrison North Pit. To bring all miners working this district into the same safety regulations, all men who worked this district came under the Louisa Lodge and it was classified as a 'gassy pit' and had to be worked with safety lamps. All three collieries had prior to nationalisation in January 1947, been owned by the South Moor Coal Co Ltd. The three collieries between them employed 1,480 men. Due to nationalisation, there had been many management changes, and at the time of the disaster the management team was as follows: J.F. Meek, manager of the Louisa, R. Peel, under manager of the Louisa and the William Pit section of the Louisa, R. Simpson, under manager of Morrison North and section of the Louisa. Mr Meek had only just taken over his post in August 1947.

A group of Bevin Boys or trainees at the Morrison.

The 4th North had a history of flooding, and that area had only recently been re-opened. Nearby was a section in the Low Main where there had been a fire in 1929 which was still burning, and held back at that time by a brick firewall, causing that area to be a safety lamp area.

The night of the disaster

Due to the great need for coal after the war, most repair work and progress was undertaken at weekends. Friday 22nd August 1947 was such an occasion, when 24 miners worked an extra shift in readiness for the following week.

The foreshift overman John Hutchinson found the ventilating system satisfactory, and free from firedamp. Deputy Maughan found no firedamp in the backshift. Deputy Hebden found no firedamp in the third shift. Overman Amos also found the district clear as late as 10.00 pm, only two hours before the explosion. Ted Errington, a blacksmith, in the area only minutes before the explosion said it was incredibly hot and humid, and that the air quality was poor.

Each of the miners involved carried an Eddison J electric cap lamp. No one carried a flame gas deflector even though required by regulations. Deputy Estelle carried a flame safety lamp. This was supposedly pointed out by Deputy Hebden. The lampman was aware of the situation but he said he was only there to hand out whatever was asked for. It is worth noting that the two deputies did the shift hand over at the surface, leaving that area underground unsupervised.

Timescale of events

7-00 pm: Johnson and Kilgallon, stonemen, descend the Louisa shaft.

10.00 pm: Bell, Chapman and Fenwick (conveyor movers) descended the Morrison North shaft reaching their place of work at 10.20 pm. Along with stonemen Appleby and Rowland who were there to take out a girder. Stonemen Simpson and Brown were there to continue a caunch along the West Face.

11.00 pm. Stonemen Bailey and Talbot descended to renew a Warrick girder. Minto and Westgarth, also stonemen, were there to complete the re-aligning of the Straight East Gate conveyor. Reed, Moore and Bell were to clean up the 2nd East Loading Gate. McKever, Roe and Martin, datal hands, were to repair the rail track on the South Heading. Hodgson, Grimley Rutherford and Birtle, stonemen, were to caunch at the 2nd East Loading Gate.

Deputy Estelle arrived just before he explosion. He had worked on the foreshift. The third shift had left the underground district at 11.00 pm, at the same time as Deputy Hebden. Deputy Estell was a little late, so Hebden had come to the surface to meet him. Hebden had already arranged with another to take charge of the district in the unlikely event of Estell not turning up.

Rescuers taking a well earned break at the Morrison North Pit. Other miners came from miles around to volunteer their services.

A local police sergeant controls the waiting crowd. Were you there? If so, let me know.

The Explosion

11.55 pm: According to Young's watch, they felt a momentary stop of intake air followed by a rush of dust from the Morrison North Shaft. Picking up their safety gear, they rushed to the area of the explosion in the 4th North District. Shanley went to phone the surface while Younger and Robinson entered the 4th North via the Straight East Gate where they found Minto unconscious. Bailey and Talbot appeared dead. Robinson went back to phone for help. Younger remained with Minto.

12.20 am. Younger discovered Bailey was still alive and went out to meet Robinson who was returning with a stretcher. Robinson then went back for breathing apparatus.

Shanley returned with foreshift Overman, J. Hutchinson who had descended the North Pit shaft at midnight. These four men showed extreme bravery as visibility was down to only a couple of feet and the air was poisonous and foul with gas fumes. The heat was tremendous. Younger and Shanley removed the three men while Robinson and Hutchinson explored the South Heading. Progress was slow.

Thomas McKever   Walter Rowe   Gerald Moore   Reg. L. Brown

Thomas Bell, New Kyo   Norman Fenwick   Joseph S. Hodgson   Thomas Bell, New. Greenside

R. Rowlands   Thos. W. Appleby   Francis E. Martin   William Reed

Some of those killed in the disaster.

A little later, all four rescuers were able to reach the South Heading up to the 2nd East Loading Point where they came across Johnson and Kilgallon, alive but unconscious. They brought them out to fresh air. By 1.30 am they had rescued Deputy Estell, alive in the area of the Kist. They brought out five bodies and located four more at the 2nd East Loading Gate. At this time they were joined by the first of the rescue team. Together they attempted to reach the Straight East Gate Loading Point, but the fumes were too heavy. The Under Manager Mr Peel arrived at this time and took charge of the rescue operation. The rescue team soon reached Westgarth with his clothes on fire just beyond the loading point. After extinguishing the fire in that area, the fumes soon dissipated. The rest of the bodies were rescued without the use of breathing apparatus.

The bodies were sent out along the two feet six inch seams in the darkness and brought up at the Morrison North Shaft where they were examined by local doctors, Fox and Josephs. They declared 19 were dead. The five survivors were transferred to Newcastle Infirmary. Local priest Rev. Cordon and Father Smith were at the pit head to administer the Last Rites. Help came in from the surrounding area and the Mine's Inspector was called in. The clothing of the bodies was examined for contraband. They found cigarettes, matches and a lighter among the possessions of eight of them.

The Mine's Inspector said it was reasonable to deduce that a Mild Firedamp Explosion, in which coal dust played no part at first, had traversed the East Face Line between the Straight East Loading Gate and the 2nd East Loading Gate. It had extended outbye along these gates and the Intermediate East Motor Board so as to open up several, separate, coal dust explosions, one in each of the gates. The most violent of these dust explosions occurred on the 2nd East Loading Gate and thus erupted violently into the South Heading. It continued to Number Four West Board opposite to the West Face Line, where it spread leftwards as far as the tailgate and to the right down Number One West Board to the South Heading. There, it died out.

On that Saturday morning, the five rescued men were taken to the Newcastle Infirmary by ambulance. Their relatives were informed and they too made their way to the hospital. Sadly, Bailey died within 24 hours. Deputy Estell managed to hang on grimly to life for several days, before he to died. The other three were nursed until they were sent home. Clement Minto had the longest fight for life. After three months of never really recovering, he sadly died. The two survivors, Johnson and Kilgallon never fully recovered the events of that fateful day. For many years only 21 were listed as being killed. At the families request, Clement Minto's name was added to the official list. For no known reason no memorial was erected to those who lost their lives until 50 years after the tragic event.

Right: *Clement Minto and family.*

The Inquest

By 1.00 pm on the Saturday, all the bodies had been recovered. That night, Coroner William Carr of Gateshead opened the Inquest on the 19 victims. Grief stricken relatives went through the ordeal of giving evidence of identification. Coroner Carr then adjourned the Inquest until September 11th. The Coroner made reference to the great bravery shown that day in the rescue.

Bevin Boys killed

Two of those killed were Bevin Boys. They were Gerald Moore of Chichester and Francis Martin of Princess Street, Catchgate. I don't know of any other Bevin Boys killed down the pit during their service, although I have been informed since that as many as eight may have been killed in the coal mining industry

Six Bevin Boys at the Morrison. Third from the right is Gerald Moore. He was killed in the 1947 explosion in the 4th North District.

Report from HM Inspector of Mines

This report from HM Inspector R. Yates was given to Parliament in March 1948. During the night shift of Friday 22nd August 1947, there was an emission of firedamp from the strata below the Hutton Seam, which created an inflammable mixture of firedamp and air on the East Face Line and the Straight East Gate. That, shortly before midnight, a Lucifer Match was struck about the Loading Point on the Straight East Gate for the purpose of lighting a cigarette, igniting this mixture and initiated a very mild firedamp explosion. This developed additional force as it progressed and was propagated by coal dust along the mechanical roadways, existing and disused, throughout the district. The explosion was finally extinguished by stone dust on the South Heading and Main Drift.

Conclusion

Once again, my conclusions are really irrelevant. However, there were many factors brought up by the Inspector that did not receive the importance it should have done. There is no question the explosion occurred due to the illegal use of matches and cigarettes underground. But, what of the facts that smoking had obviously been allowed to happen over a long period of time in that district, and obviously in the knowledge of the management, due to the fact many spent matches were discovered in the area named 'The Kist'. You could not smoke here with at least the deputies and overmen knowing. Also, there was coal dust lying thickly in many areas, and also over a long period of time. This was against colliery regulations. There was also some misuse of the canvass doors, also against colliery regulations. The management appear to have got off very lightly.

Rescuers and families at Buckingham Palace to receive MBEs.

Most of this account is from 'A Disaster Waiting To Happen' by Jack Hair.

The Memorial Service in 1997

I saw an article in the local paper saying this disaster had no memorial stone to those who lost their lives. It was by Tom (Wilkie) Burleigh who had gifted a prize in the name of the disaster for a bowls competition. I had not been aware of this and decided to look into it. In no time at all, I had persuaded my friend Ron Hindhaugh and the Rev Jeff Laws of St Aidan's Church, Annfield Plain that we could raise sufficient funds to erect such a memorial. It went so well, that within weeks we had sufficient to erect a granite memorial in the grounds of St Aidan's. We placed it here to avoid the lengthy planning regulations. A service was arranged, and we informed through the press as many relatives of those killed as we could.

The Bishop of Durham, the Rt Rev David Jenkins performed the service assisted by other local clergy. Annfield Plain Gleemen and Langley Park Colliery band were also part of this very moving service. Several of the widows of those killed attended and they and their families were really grateful that after all these years, their loved ones had been recognised as paying the ultimate price in the quest for coal.

Above: *The Memorial stone dedicated at St Aidan's on August 23rd 1997.*

Right: *The Memorial Service of Dedication at St Aidan's Church.*

John Pattison – East Stanley Poet

Some time ago, my friend Michael Bailey was handed an old crumpled book which he was given by a care worker at East Stanley. It had been thrown into a skip on the estate. This old book was the hand written notes of John Pattison. It contained many local history accounts, plus a large selection of poems John had compiled during his short life. He was obviously an admirer of the work of Tommy Armstrong, the Pitman's Poet, and his poetry was based on mostly factual accounts of events of his day. Some was very humorous, while others were tinged with the sadness of him having a serious spine injury while working at Beamish Colliery.

Following is a brief account of John Pattison and a mention of just some of his poems. I personally think very highly of his work, and for that reason, I had some of it made up into a book, and Durham County Council Library Service published it but only a few copies were made because it was made in hard back. The county book number is:

CO 1 56 30807 C2.

John was born in 1870 and died in 1909, aged 38. His father was born in Wagtail Cottages at Craghead in 1843. His mother, Mary was believed to be born in the Robin Hood public House. In 1852 John was born in Scotts Houses, Stanley on 9th October 1870. These houses were directly behind what is now the Empire club on Front Street. He had a sister born in Joicey Square and then the family appear to have moved to Long Horsley where another five brothers and sisters were born. They then moved back to East Stanley where three more siblings were born, the last being Alfred in 1895.

John's father died in 1914 aged 70. His mother died in 1911. John died on 13th February 1909 three days before the Burns Pit Disaster. According to my research notes of John in 1998, I recorded the strong possibility of his family being related to the Rodham family and Hilary Rodham Clinton, wife of former President of the USA, Bill Clinton. I am unable to retrace my notes due to my very poor eyesight. There must have been strong evidence or I would not have noted it.

Also, when I wrote the book, I dedicated it to the late Michael Bailey, who sadly died before I was able to complete it. Michael, a founder member of Stanley Past & Present, was himself a keen poet.

Some of the poems John compiled were as follows: Misfortune, The Military Band, Pat At The Races, The Beamish Jail, the Monster Turkey, A Day At The Empire, The Old Folks Treat, Sanger's Circus 1905, The Stanley Band Contest, The Wag At The Wall, The Unhappy Couple, and many more.

Misfortune by John Pattison

When off the bourd for fourteen years
One finds he's out of date
Its precious small he sees or hears
His is an awful fate

Just imagine being buried alive
By tons of falling stones
The result is a thousand and five
Times warse than broken bones

The verdict is an injured spine
A life long miser(y)ee
No one knows while down the mine
Who next it is to be

He cannot make a single move
Without someone's assistance
Oh would some power from above
Relieve such cruel existence

Such is the case of scores of men
Misfortune has afflicted
Nine cases out of every ten
Have come quite unpredicted.

Kind friends we have and friends we need
That give consideration
They cheer us up by word and deed
On more than one occasion

Yet we long to take part
In sport and recreation
And longs to test old nature's art
The joy of all sensation

Although we wish, we wish in vain
For pleasures are denied
Then be content to sing to Him
Abide with me, Abide

Good luck to all unfortunate friends
My wish it is sincere
That each a Merry Christmas spends
And a downright, Happy New Year

Oakey's Pit
West Shield Row Colliery

Local historian, Fred Wade lists this colliery as opening in 1854. It was worked for some years before closing down. It was then re-opened by the Dickinson family in 1869 according to Wade and re-named West Shield Row Colliery. It was later taken over by the South Derwent Coal Co, although the name Oakey's had remained as the local name for this colliery. There were five seams of coal worked here, namely, the Main Coal, Hutton, the Busty, Brockwell and later the Victoria. There was an upcast shaft 300 yards to the east sunk in 1856. This capped shaft was later found and had the

letters, C.E.O. A.D. 1856. The CEO stood for the original owner, Charles Edward Oakey. The annual output in later years was 150,000 tons which went via the Louisa. There were at one time 328 employees. There was a fire on 30th October 1909 which destroyed the wooden headgear and heapstead, as shown in the photo on the left. All the surface works were rebuilt with steel. The colliery closed on 9th November 1934. Amazingly, even the local playing fields still bear the name of Oakey's after all these years.

Oakey's Cottages were demolished circa 1934/35 although some people say they remember them even after that date. These were very basic dwellings as were many of the early miner's cottages. It was only when the mine owners realised just how much coal there was underground, did they decide to build larger, more comfortable housing. They needed the miners and their

families to stay and knew if they stayed, they would also get their children to work down the mines. It wasn't a gesture of kindness. Just a way of maintaining their labour force.

Tommy Armstrong worked at Oakey's for many years as a coal hewer. A Keeker named Joseph Elliott was transferred from Annfield Plain to Oakeys. He originally lived at Maiden Law. He was known by most as 'Maiden Law Joe'. He was a little over zealous when checking the tubs for excess stone. If a tub had more than the permitted amount of stone it was 'Laid Out'. The miner was not paid for that tub of coal. The miner would only get to know when he returned to bank if any of his tubs had been laid out. He soon became unpopular with the coal hewers. Tommy had many a row with Joe, and eventually wrote the song 'Oakey's Keeker' saying what he thought about Maiden Law Joe. The Keeker was so upset, he took out a summons for slander against Tommy Armstrong, but it was refused by the Lanchester Magistrates.

Shield Row Drift

A strange name for a coal mine nearer to Quaking Houses than South Moor. It was situated south of the Charlie Pit. Coals from here travelled to the south pit surface on the north landing, and along to the Louisa Colliery. On the photo below the small building on the left was the lamp cabin. The larger building in the centre was the manager's office and ambulance room, with the canteen nearby. At the top left of the photo is the end of the Drift Cottages. At one time, these were occupied by the Platten family and the Shield family. When the colliery closed, many of the men transferred to Fenhall Drift.

F. Weber with his pit pony at Shield Row Drift.

T. Dodds also with his pit pony at Shield Row Drift.

Many men from Shield Row Drift transferred to Fenhall Drift after closure around 1952/53. On this photograph is F. Webber, amongst others, at Stanley with Fenhall Lodge and banner.

Stanhope & Tyne Railway

The biggest single reason for the coal industry making such huge progress in North West Durham, was undoubtedly, the ingenuity and inventiveness of those who found ways of transporting the coal in amounts sufficient to make it a worthwhile venture. Standing steam haulage engines and the incline waggonways were brought inland in the form of the Stanhope & Tyne Railway. This allowed a continuous flow of coal and limestone from Weardale and North Durham down to the coast where it could be shipped anywhere it was needed.

The company was formed in 1831 with the capital sum of £200,000. The consulting engineer was Robert Stephenson with Thomas E. Harrison as acting engineer. The railway was just short of 38 miles in length from Stanhope to Tyne Dock in South Shields. There was an original plan to route it through what was the existing Shield Row Waggonway but Major Swinburne refused a right of way. There was great competition between the varying groups of coal owners at this time, so they opted for the route through West Stanley. This very probably influenced the sinking of West Stanley Colliery by Burns & Clark. The final route chosen was from Stanhope Lime Quarries to Weatherhill, Cold Rowley, Howens Gill, Carr House,

Stanley Bank Head, from where self acting incline sent coal down to Pelton Level.

Leadgate, East Castle, Annfield Plain, West Stanley, Fatfield, Washington, Boldon Lane to Laings Dock at South Shields. Work commenced at Stanhope in 1832 and at South Shields in 1833. There was no single contractor. The work was carried out by various groups, each on their own section of the railway. The landscape caused several problems with the hilly layout of some sections causing a different approach to each section. Some were able to work with steam powered standing engines, while others were by way of incline planes. Howens Gill proved very difficult with an 800 feet ravine. They solved this by hauling the wagons up one side and lowering them down the other with a 20 horse power steam engine located at the bottom of the ravine. A special device was introduced so as to take the wagons in and out of this very steep ravine. They were only able to transport over the Gill 12 wagons an hour.

The upper part of the line from Stanhope to Annfield Plain was opened on 15th May 1834, a distance of 15¼ miles. Most of this journey was by stationary engine and horses with a very short distance by gravity.

The lower section of the line opened on 10th September 1834. The first section known as Stanley Level was worked by horses to Stanley Bank Head and then by self acting inclines down to Pelton.

Stella Bridge to South Stanley. Prior to the building of this bridge, such was the rail traffic, it was almost impossible to cross without great danger.

On 10th September 1834, 100 wagons of Medomsley coal was sent down towards Fox's Quarry near the Barnes, and taken on to The Drops, and loaded onto a small brig named 'Sally'.

Apart from the lime kilns at Stanhope, there were also some at East Castle. Coal from East Castle pit was used at these kilns, using up to 10,000 tons of coal per annum. After 1839, the company ceased to manufacture lime. In 1840, 510,000 tons of coal were conveyed on this railway to the Tyne. By 1842, it was discovered its liabilities were twice what the company was worth and the company was dissolved and a new system set in its place.

The western section was sold to the Derwent Iron Co down to Leadgate. Also in 1842, the eastern section became the Pontop & South Shields Railway by Act of Parliament on 4th May of that year. In 1845, it was sold to George Hudson for £450,000. In 1863, from Howens Gill to Shields was absorbed by the Stockton & Darlington Railway who had taken over the Wear Valley Line. A new section of line was opened in 1866 between Kyo Laws and East Castle, cutting out the Loud Hill engine.

The company was taken over by NER and the LNER. In recent years, there have been moves to restore part of the old lime kilns at East Castle. All that is left of that village is a short street of the former railway workmen's houses, now a horse riding establishment and the public house, now a private dwelling.

South Moor Arch. Originally constructed of stone. Though no longer still standing, this location is still named locally, 'The Arch'.

South Tanfield Colliery, Oxhill

Another oddly named colliery. It was situated just to the west of Oxhill Rail Crossings at the top of Quaking House Hill. I have no photo of this colliery but the map shows its location, and also the fact it was a fairly large colliery. The colliery was sunk and opened in 1837 and closed in 1915. There were three shafts. The A shaft was sunk in 1837; the B shaft in 1838; and the C shaft in 1880 at which time, one of the sinkers, T. Davison fell to his death. The annual tonnage was about 250,000 tons. The most men employed was in 1896 with 607 men. At least six seams were worked here. Note Quaking House at bottom of map.

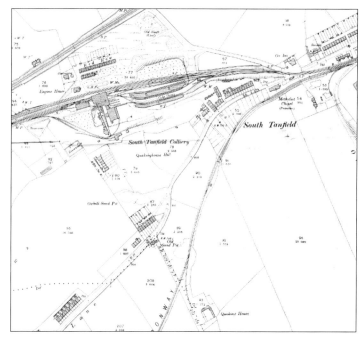

Left: South Tanfield Colliery Band was probably one of the first formed in the district, pictured here near the colliery.

Tanfield Moor Colliery

This colliery was situated between Tantobie and White-le-Head. It was opened in 1768 for the Earl of Kerry. By 1810 the owner was William Pitt and there were four seams working. It was taken over in the 1850s by James Joicey and again in the 1940s by Lambton, Hetton and Joicey. The NCB took it over in 1947 but closed it in the same year. Pits named were Conquest, Mount and Willie. Employment was highest in 1902 with 365 men. The seams worked were Main Seam, Brass Thill, Hutton, Five Quarter, Main Coal and Hutton Bottom and Shield Row. This colliery was classed as the oldest deep coalmine in the district.

In 1887, John Green aged 53, a horsekeeper was crushed to his death by a cage in the shaft. William Keelor, aged 42 in 1925, was decapitated when he was run over by a set of trucks.

There was a wagon way from this colliery, down through Tanfield Lea to the Causey. The outline can still be seen today from behind the Ice Cream Factory opposite the old Wagon Inn.

This is supposedly miners on strike digging for coal at Mountsett Fell. A lady from Marley Hill wrote to me saying the man with the gloves on was her father, and that they were Marley Hill miners.

Tanfield Lea Colliery

This colliery opened in 1829 and closed in August 1962. Pits named were the Anne Pit, Bute Pit and Engine Pit, although the name that comes to mind most to me was the Margaret Pit pictured below, and the North Pit. The highest number of men employed seems to have been 1914 with 1,469 men. Seams worked were the Brass Thill, Five Quarter, Hutton, Main, Wind, Margaret, Beaumont, Brockwell, Top and Bottom Busty, Tilley and Victoria, The Engine Shaft was sunk in 1829. A second shaft 600 yards away was sunk in 1839. In 1898, the Wind Pit was sunk down to the Victoria Seam. In 1903, the Margaret Shaft was being sunk. Tanfield Lea Colliery workers had their own Welfare Hall and Welfare Park as shown in later photos.

Margaret Pit, Tanfield Lea.

Right: The Margaret Pit – one of my favourite photos in my collection.

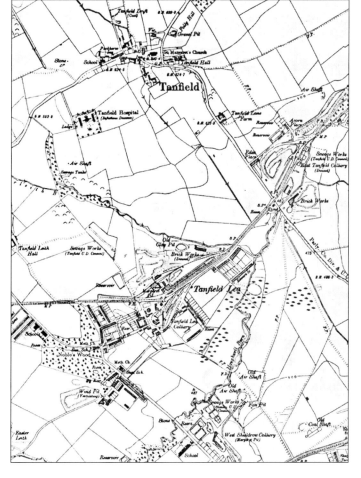

Early photo of Tanfield Lea Colliery.

Tanfield Lea Colliery Baths.

Left: A 1920s map of Tanfield Lea.

Left: A proud day for Tanfield Lea Colliery Lodge when they marched into the Durham Miners' Gala with the United States 751 Air Force Band. It didn't half make people look at Tanfield Lea. The band also gave a marching exhibition and music in Murray Park, Stanley for the local people later in the weekend. A huge photo of this is in Tanfield Lea Working Men's Club. This band created so much interest, yet this is the only photograph I have seen up to now. Do you have any photos of their time with Tanfield lea Lodge? If so, I would love to see them.

Right: Tanfield Lea North Pit, 1960.

Left: Mechanics and engineering staff from Tanfield Lea Colliery. The only person I can name is Jackie Stobbart who is the tall lad in the middle of the back row.

Two views of Tanfield Lea Lodge Banner. Including: G. Armstrong, J. Fisher, T. Robson, C. Bartell, J. Stephens, C. Brannen, W. Pratt, A. Grundy, T. Rockett, T. Watkins, W. Holden. I have misplaced the names of the two men on the poles, sorry.

Opening of Tanfield Lea Colliery Welfare Park. This park was handed over to the local authority, but like many others, it was allowed to fall into disrepair.

Above: Soup kitchens at William Street during an early strike. William and George Streets were supposedly made of wood. My mother lived here as a child and her father was a knocker up for the men on the early shifts.

Right: Tanfield Lea Lodge back from the Miners' Gala in the 1940s on Stanley Front Street.

Left: A group of Tanfield Lea deputies away on a trip for the day.

West Stanley Colliery
The Burns Pit

This colliery, situated on the southern area of the present King's Head Field, was sunk by Messrs. Burns & Clark in 1832. It is thought the owners picked this particular site for its proximity to the proposed Stanhope & Tyne Railway. At the time of sinking, most of the land surrounding the colliery was a plantation of trees interspersed with some grazing land and some quarries. Also nearby was Stanley Hall, an old Manor House.

West Stanley Lodge Banner.

West Stanley Colliery Explosion
19th April 1882 – 13 killed

On the 19th April 1882, an underground explosion in the Busty Seam of West Stanley Colliery resulted in the deaths of 13 miners. Five men were rescued.

Those killed: Robert Hunter (Master Shifter), Thomas Curry (Deputy), Thomas Coulson Back Overman, John Westgarth, William Turner, Henry Turner, J.S. Clark, John Clark, John Douglas, James McCabe, Robert Hutchinson, W.J. Riley and Thomas Johnson.

The survivors were: James Kelly, John Nicholson, William Grigor, James Lowrey and William Charlton.

Fortunately, there was little damage to the Busty Shaft and rescue work commenced almost immediately. The explosion occurred at approx. 1.00 am. The rescuers, held back by the after damp reached the first of the men just after the forenoon and the five rescued were taken immediately to bank. The existence of the after damp and damage caused by the explosion made progress slow. News of the explosion was sent to the County Assistant Inspector of Mines, Mr Atkinson who entered the underground workings with Mr W. Johnson, the Resident Viewer, and a Mr Bell. Ten of the dead men were found and it was considered the remaining three could not have survived in that area of the pit. All of the horses and ponies, except one, died in the explosion. Several of the miner's bodies were very disfigured. The cause of the explosion was unknown. The workmen in the mine had safety lamps with them, but they were locked. Two men were engaged in firing shots, but as they were both found at the bottom of the shaft, evidently having done their work, the accident is not ascribed to this cause. One of the men was found alive, but died before he reached the surface. Mr Burn, the owner, sent word that no money had to be spared in the rescue work. This extract was taken from an edition of *The Times* from 20th April 1882.

Details from a Report by Arnold Morley MP on an Inquiry into the explosion:

The Coroner opened an inquest into the deaths the following day and adjourned it until 25th, 26th and 27th May 1882 resulting in the following findings:

The causes of death were as stated by Dr Benson.

The Busty Seam was declared in safe working order immediately prior to the men descending on the day of the disaster.

The accident was deemed to have occurred in the Busty Seam in the area where McCabe was working.

The explosion is believed to have been caused by the quick movement of a safety lamp.

No one was held responsible for the explosion.

Mr John Edge appeared on behalf of the owners.

Mr Bowey represented the Miners' National Union.

Mr Heaviside represented the Durham Miners' Union.

Mr Thomas Bell and Mr James Willis represented Her Majesty's Inspector of Mines along with Mr Atkinson, Assistant Inspector to Mr Bell and all took part in the examination of witnesses. Mr Arnold Morley, the author of the inquiry represented the Secretary of State during the three days of the adjourned Inquest.

Twenty three witnesses were questioned at the Inquest, including the officials who had inspected the mines shortly before the men had gone underground, plus a miner from another area of the pit and scientific witnesses.

At the date of the explosion, the following were the officials of the colliery:

George Greenwell, Consultant Viewer.
William Johnson, Manager and Resident Viewer.
William Anderson, Overman and Wasteman.
Thomas J. Coulson, Back Overman.
Robert Hunter, Master Shifter.

Two of those listed above, Coulson and Hunter were among those listed killed in the explosion. There were two deputies and an average of 25 coal hewers in each shift.

West Stanley Colliery.

William Johnson had been the Manager of the colliery for five years with virtual control of the mine as the Consulting Viewer, Mr Greenwell, only visited the colliery once a month. In several important particulars concerning the mine, the management appeared to be defective, with evidence of decided irregularities. Both with the provisions laid down by the Mines Regulations Act, and with reference to the ordinary precautions which should in every case, be taken. It appears from reading the account, the Manager did not totally accept the colliery was a fiery pit, and as such did not demand all the necessary precautions be taken, within the meaning of the Mines Regulations Act 1872, and less care appeared to have been taken than probably would have been the case had it been fully realised that considerable danger must exist in any mine where gas was so frequently discovered as had been the case in the Busty Seam. Records seem to have been less important than should have been. One deputy was unable to read. Mr Johnson, the manager said he had never seen a copy of the said rules in his five years as manager. The deputy said if gas was ever detected, it was dealt with by altering the position of the brattice or some other way. The officials had a very imperfect knowledge of the rules, and did not appreciate, their responsibility of their position. What records there were, were kept at the Manager's house, some distance from the colliery. Other records relating to the pit lamps were also very poor. Two of four of the pit lamps found at the scene at the South Crosscuts were found to be unlocked. Either the lampman had handed over the lamps unlocked, or the men themselves had broken the rules and opened them for some reason. The list of rules not carried out correctly seemed quite long and suggested everything was not as it should have been.

I have only found one memorial. That of Thomas Hepple Curry, aged 30, of 111 Burns Houses. He was buried at St Andrew's Churchyard. He left a wife and two children.

West Stanley Colliery Disaster (The Burns Pit)
I6th February 1909
168 men and boys killed in an underground explosion

I cover this disaster from various sources, the main one being the Report from the Inspector of Mines to the Government. This report also covered the Inquests. The result of this Inquest left a lot to be desired, and has been considered controversial for many years. I do however, state that I am not in a position to question any of the evidence given. I only give my opinion and it is up to the individual to research the subject themselves, and make up their own mind. The inspector's report is so long, I am only able to give a summary in this book.

On Tuesday 16th February 1909 at 3.45 pm, there was an explosion at West Stanley Colliery in North Durham. About 50 seconds later, there was a second explosion ripping through the headgear with flames shooting into the sky. It was obvious there was serious trouble underground. Thousands of people headed to the colliery and they were in for a long wait into the next day before the first of the 30 survivors were brought to the surface. There had been 198 men and boys underground, but only thirty went home alive. For many years, there have been lengthy discussions as to the use of illegal lamps underground. These stories took their origin from the fact the former manager Mr Hall, gave a lecture at a local library and displayed a Howart's Patent Deflector Lamp which he said came out of the Burns Pit after the disaster. He later donated this

Colliery Where Accident Occurred West Stanley

lamp to the Armstrong Mining Museum in Newcastle. This particular lamp was illegal in gassy pits, and the Burns was registered as a gassy pit due to previous explosion. I will try to give both sides, but I lean toward the theory of the illegal use of lamps as a possible cause of this explosion.

The scene at the pit after the explosion.

Report to His Majesty's Government 1909 By R.A.S. Redmayne, Chief Inspector of Mines and R.D. Bain, HM Inspector of Mines

On hearing of the explosion, Inspector Bain and assistants Walker and Charlton proceeded to the colliery and stayed for the removal of the bodies and to explore the workings. Mr R.S.A. Redmayne, Chief Inspector of Mines and Electrical Inspector of Electricals R. Nelson arrived the next day and took part in the exploration from time to time.

Moving to the Inquest

The Inquests opened on 18th February 1909 by Coroner J. Graham at St Andrew's Church Institute, Stanley. The inquest was adjourned from time to time for the identification of bodies as they were brought to the surface, and take medical evidence as to cause of death of the 166 miners found. This was of course 165 plus the man who died after some 30 hours. Two bodies were unrecovered at that time.

The main inquest resumed on 29th March. Their first task was to ascertain the condition of the colliery prior to the men going underground. Representatives from all the relevant organisations were present with their legal advisors. This part of the Inquest lasted three days. Coroner Graham summed up after 10 days deliberation and left 19 questions for the jury answer.

To summarise, the jury decided:

The causes of death were as those given by the Medical Officer.

Towneley, Tilley, Busty and Brockwell Seams were all deemed as good working order and all precautions taken.

Downcast and upcast shafts, plus ventilation all deemed as in good condition and working order. Lamps issued in good condition and locked. Electrics and materials all satisfactory and safe.

All officials and staff experienced and competent, and all rules complied to.

Explosion occurred in Busty Seam.

Makeshift coffins at the joiners' shop.

There was probably just one explosion.

The explosion occurred Busty Seam between curve and crossing.

It was a dust explosion.

Jury unable to find cause of explosion.

No one was found culpable.

Jury unable to find cause of dust explosion.

The jury had no recommendations to make to the owners.

Atherley Jones thanked the Coroner for his handling of the Inquest and went on to thank the rescuers and also the owner.

Atherley Jones thanked the coroner for his handling of the Inquest. He also thanked the rescuers for their efforts and the owners for their generosity to those affected by the disaster.

A trench grave at the Town Cemetery adjacent to St Andrew's Church.

Colliery Seams passed through by the shafts

Shield Row Seam at 39 fathoms.
Five Quarter Seam at $52^{1}/_{2}$ fathoms.
Brass Thill at 67 fathoms.
Low Main Seam at 93 fathoms.
Towneley Seam at 134 fathoms. Coal 2 feet 2 inches.
Busty Seam at 139 fathoms. Coal 3 feet.
Brockwell Seam at 163 fathoms. Coal 2 feet 5 inches.

Officials Underground

Manager J.P. Hall. Under Manager R. Heslop.
Two Fore Overmen, one Back Overman.
Two Master Shifters, 22 Deputies.
527 men and boys underground.
118 men and boys on surface.

Two photographs showing the scene at the Town Cemetery.

Lamps

There were 20 incandescent electric lights in the Busty Seam.
15 incandescent electric lights in the Towneley Seam.
637 Masaut safety lamps.
111 Donald type.

All lamps lighted and locked by lead rivets in lamproom at the surface prior to going underground. No re-lighting was allowed underground. All extinguished lamps were returned to the surface. The oil used was Calza and Petroleum Homelight.

The Explosion – Possible origin and cause

The inspectors could not say exactly just where the explosion occurred, and this has been an ongoing contention over the years. The Government Inspectors gave great importance to what they considered the eye witness account of one of the survivors. This witness, suffering from a serious concussion and ill in his bed at home, was questioned by the coroner in his bedroom with all the inspectors and representatives also present. He was asked questions with the answers almost attached to the questions and answered yes to most of them. I do not for one moment suggest the answers were lies, I only think this today would not have been allowed. I will later give an account of the independent highly qualified inspectors who mostly disagreed with the findings of the government inspectors, all to no avail.

The funeral procession in Stanley.

Inspectors' Observations

The inspectors discounted any thoughts of the Tilley Seam being the source of the explosion. Their first thoughts appear to have pointed to the Towneley Seam where they had believed the source of the explosion may have been close to the shaft, at the haulage engine house. However, after a report by the electrical inspector that there was no evidence of electrical faults, this theory was discounted. They moved next to the Brockwell Seam which had evidence of actual burning. The position of the bodies suggested they had received no warning of the explosion, and also their lamps were filled with coal dust to a depth of half an inch. These circumstances made most of the inspectors believe this was the source of the explosion, but it was discounted because of the statement there was no source (naked light) and that all lamps were legal safety lamps. This of course only left the Busty Seam and even the inspectors could not come up with any explainable cause. This is just a brief account, as the actual document is many pages long.

Concluding Observations from Inspector of Mines

'It appears fairly certain that a small initial explosion – a mere puff – was succeeded within 50 seconds by a much more extensive and severe explosion which did practically all the damage, and which was projected from seam to seam. Where either of these explosions happened, we are not prepared to say, but clearly, it was not in the Tilley Seam. The main explosion may have been initiated by an explosion of gas, but was undoubtedly propagated by coal dust. What the means of ignition, we cannot say. We are anxious to emphasise the impression made upon us in investigating this and other explosions, that unless the grave danger which exists at many collieries owing to the presence of coal dust is attacked with much greater earnestness in the future, than it has been in the past, disasters of a similar character will occur from time to time.

'There is one feature of the case to which we have not yet alluded, but to which we are desirous of directing attention, namely the inability of those concerned with the management of the colliery to make any but a very wide estimate of the number of persons underground at the time of the explosion. It was at first supposed that these were under 100, and it was not until nearly all the bodies had been recovered several days after the explosion, that a correct estimate was arrived at. We directed our cross examination of the lampman, John Todd, to elucidating for the reason for this, and he gave us in explanation the fact that the spare lamps were sent out regularly from the mine to be relit, and that the numbers in consequence got confused. There was no system of tokens or tallies in vogue at the colliery. Were each man to hand a token with his number to the banksman, before entering the cage to descend the mine and receive it back on arriving at the surface, it would it would be possible to determine at any moment of the day, the number of persons below ground. Some such system is in operation at some collieries, and is easily worked. The register which is required to be kept under the Eight Hours Act, will however obviate all uncertainty in future.'

A lone boy standing amongst floral tributes at St Joseph's Churchyard.

He then went on to thank all those who

had helped after the explosion and those involved in the inquiry. It is the next piece which is ironical.

'It is gratifying to be able to state that throughout a long and exhaustive inquiry, no breach of the Coal Mines' Act or Special Rules was brought to light.'

This may well have been an honest statement at this time by the inspector. However, at a later date, it was disclosed illegal lamps were in the Brockwell Seam at the time of the explosion. This fact would have been known by at least some of the management, deputies up over.

Crowds flocked to Stanley to pay their respects.

If they knew, they should have said so at the inquiry, which would have made it more evident, the explosion probably began, as then thought, in the Brockwell Seam. But, it's too late now, and as I said, it's only my opinion.

Eric Forester's excellent book *The Death Pit* goes into much greater detail and I would advise any interested person to read it. Atkinson, the Mining Inspector also went to great lengths to promote this theory for many years and there was great talk of conspiracy at very high levels. Atkinson's notes are also available.

I have covered this subject now for many years even going into local primary schools as part of their curriculum. I have written a book on the subject and produced powerpoint presentations and a narrated dvd. With my colleague Bob Drake, we arranged a Centenary Service of Tribute to those killed in this disaster. It is now time for me to move on. This will probably be my last account or mention of this terrible day in our history, but, we should never forget the huge price the coal miners paid in the quest for coal.

Temporary Hospital cum Mortuary

While the rescuers were repairing the shafts to gain entry to the seams below, other workers were converting the Joiner Shops into a temporary hospital cum mortuary. As it turned out, the hospital was only used for three men, one from the Busty Seam and two from the Towneley. These men were brought up by the downcast shaft. Twenty-six were rescued from the Tilley Seam. Of the others, John Smith, Patrick Cogan, Robert Leadbitter and last man rescued Patrick Joyce were from the Towneley Seam while Onsetter Matt Elliott was from the Busty Seam. Robert Leadbitter died of his injuries within 30 hours. Concerning Patrick Cogan, the inspector's report is the only place I have seen this man's name mentioned. I find that most unusual. If you are related to him or have any further information, please let me know. There is a fuller account of the hospital later on in the brief account of *The Death Pit*.

There are several discrepancies between how the Inspector of Mines saw the situation to that of other independent witnesses. I don't know which was correct.

In Loving and Affectionate Remembrance of

The Miners who lost
their lives in the

STANLEY PIT EXPLOSION

Which occured at West Stanley, on February 16th, 1909, resulting in over 150 deaths.

Oh, cruel the terrible stroke,
That took their dear life's breath away,
Little dreamt they that time was the last,
When they left home to toil that day

Left: A card produced to raise money for a memorial fund.

82

Brief summary of 'The Death Pit'

The Death Pit was a book by Evening Chronicle reporter Eric Forster who sadly died some years ago.

For people like myself, this was the most detailed book of independent witnesses available concerning this disaster. The general gist of the events were the same with some rather glaring differences in important interpretations of events.

Forster says concerning the first explosion, there was the sound of a dull explosion, similar to thunder rumbling in the hills heard throughout the town. Inspector Redmayne described it as no more than a mere puff. Stephenson also stated that the three sides of the shaft were blown off. This was before the second explosion. Engineer Stephenson stated that the fuses were blown indicating the ventilation had been cut off underground. The Inspector of Electricals said no fuses were blown. At the inquest, Redmayne give only in his report the accounts of those favourable to how he himself assessed the situation. He makes no reference to French Mining Engineer Delessops or Mining Inspector Atkinson who totally disagreed with his findings. They were both convinced the explosion occurred in the Brockwell Seam most probably by some form of naked light. Others were leaning in this direction if it had not been stressed most strongly there were no infringements in the colliery regarding any lamps other than safety lamps being in use. This

The band leads the way on lower Front Street.

turned out to be untrue when the manager Mr Hall later showed a lamp taken from the Brockwell Seam after the disaster – A Howatt's Patent Deflector Lamp. He showed this lamp at a lecture at Annfield Plain Library some time after the disaster. He then donated the lamp to the Armstrong Mining Museum at Newcastle. So even though there is no evidence this lamp, or others like it caused the explosion, it could have. It also meant witnesses had given false statements, concerning illegal lamps, and you can only ask the question, 'Why?' The Inspector suggests the men of the Tilley Seam survived because there was little damage in that area and that the men were a long way from the shaft. He makes no mention to the great bravery and knowledge of coal mining used by the Deputy, Mark Henderson, which resulted in the saving of these 26 men. The questioning of Matt Elliott, obviously very seriously injured in his bed by those of the inquest jury and officials left a lot to be desired. He was ill in his bed for some considerable time. He should have been allowed to recover. His evidence may have been the same, but at the time of quite robust and suggestive questioning, he was seriously concussed and suffering from gas poisoning.

Stephenson gave his account of going from the engine house over to the North Shaft. He said, the doors were hanging off and that the woods were blown off three sides of the shaft. He peered down into the belly of the pit, and there was a red glow. As he looked down, the glow grew brighter as if it was a volcano waiting to erupt. He stood back to shout a warning, when the fire leapt up through the headgear, with flames shooting into the wintry sky. He was thrown to his side and the heat seared his cheeks. The flames were followed by dense black foul smoke and his world was darkened. After sometime, the smoke was sucked back down into the pit until his vision was clear again. He was the nearest to the scene of the disaster.

I myself have interviewed several people who have been in an explosion. Ninety per cent of them had no recollection whatsoever of the explosion itself. The only one who did only had a very vague recollection. Yet, the Inquest inquiry of Elliott even got him to make statements as to direction of blast, lights and other events in detail. Yet again, I am not saying I am right. I am only giving my opinion that it may stretch the imagination a little to expect a man so seriously injured to remember all this in detail, or was he led by clever questioning?

Since the disaster, Inspector Atkinson made many attempts to have the Inquest reopened to no avail. There were articles in the press as to a conspiracy of silence. Men on high seemed to close ranks so as to prevent any reopening of the Inquest. As I have said several times. I do not know what happened or which events were true or if there was

A West Stanley disaster memorial card.

any conspiracy. However, after almost twenty years researching this subject from time to time, I tend to lean toward the account of *The Death Pit* by Forster. If you can read this book, do so.

Left: William Gardner, one of the survivors rescued from the West Stanley disaster.

84

A selection from the four memorials in the town to the West Stanley Colliery Disaster.

Left: This memorial was funded by the working men's clubs of Stanley & District and was erected outside Stanley Urban District Council Offices on Stanley Front Street. It was unveiled on 15th February 1913 by Mr B.T. Hall, Secretary to the Working Men's Clubs Institute. The memorial cost £130. It stayed on this site until 1936, when it was removed to the entrance of the Town Cemetery at East Stanley, where it still stands today.

Above: The third memorial on the site of the shaft erected by Stanley Hall Partnership.

Above: The second memorial is sited on Stanley King's Head Field. Mr Michael Bailey was the fund organiser and was assisted by Michael Brough, Derek Little and Joe Tyers, plus South Moor Police. He was also aided by Kevin Keegan who arranged a charity match with Newcastle United and a local team. The memorial was unveiled on 16th February 1995 by Kevin Keegan at 3.45 pm (the time of the explosion).

Left: The fourth memorial is sited at No 1 Trench Grave in the former Town Cemetery adjacent to St Andrew's Church. It was dedicated by the Bishop of Jarrow after a service at St Andrew's on Saturday 5th March 2005. The total cost was £5,581.21p.

A service was held at St Andrew's Church, Stanley, on Saturday 14th February 2009. Over 600 people attended with the church filled to capacity.

Above: Mrs Betty Wall and son Alan from Essex with Jack Hair at United Reform Church after the Centenary Service.

Right: The Bishop of Jarrow, Rt Rev Mark Bryant.

Craghead Colliery Band and the Annfield Plain Gleemen at the service.

The Tanfield Lea Banner at St Andrews.

Bob Drake giving the first reading.

A miner's lamp hanging in St Andrew's Chancel.

Members of the Annfield Plain Gleemen.

William Pit
Old South Moor

The William Pit was sunk by Hedley in 1839. It was originally named, West Craghead Colliery. A waggonway was built from the colliery up to Oxhill and standing haulage engines were used to haul the coal up to Oxhill, before the coal was transported through Stanley. After the closure of Oxhill Engine, the coal was transported underground to the Hedley Pit and then on up to the Louisa Colliery. The first houses for this colliery were at High and Low Rows. There were also a group of houses called 'The Barracks'. Bricks were used from the brickworks at Craghead Colliery. These were all very basic, and only improved when it was realised the vast amounts of coal available underground. The first school was on Wagtail Lane, between Quaking Houses and Craghead, followed in 1900 by the Old Moor School. The Colliery Lodge closed in 1962. The following photos refer to both the William and Hedley Collieries, as they shared offices and band.

Above: Two views of the William Pit.

Right: South Moor loco worked between South Moor and the Morrison. Have you any pit photos? Let me know. Why not visit my website www.stanley-codurham-jackhair.com

Miners' Welfare Hall at South Moor. It had reading rooms, library, snooker hall and dance hall.

Old colliery offices and workshops at Quaking Houses.

Holmside & South Moor Welfare Fund Hospital. The first patient is believed to have been my uncle, Baden Powell Hair.

Former South Moor Colliery Policemen, Stubbs and Vittee. They had a huge area to cover and their job was not made easy because for some years there were no regulated opening hours in the local pubs. It was a hard job to keep the peace. There was not even an age limit for many years. The law was only changed because so many men were losing work due to the drink.

Derby Day Rail Mishap at South Moor, 1920

For whatever reasons, the driver lost control of the engine at South Moor, near the coal depot and the loco came off the rails. The boiler was sent away for repair to Hawthorn Leslie at Hebburn and later returned to South Moor. I have several photos of this event.

Hedley Colliery, South Moor

The Hedley Colliery was opened in 1885. There were two shafts side by side. The seams worked were the Five Quarter, Main Coal and Shield Row. In the 1920s, a whole shift of men were trapped underground when the two shafts were damaged. The men had to be rescued from the small escape tower erected on Kitley Nook, near Ashley Park. The wooden steps leading to the building were so rotten, only a few men at a time could be brought up. The rescue took until the next day. A marquee had been erected for the waiting relatives. There was another event which resulted when 19 of the Hedley men were awarded the Edward Medal for their bravery in rescuing a fellow miner.

Above: The Hedley Pit.

The coal from the Hedley was sent by wagon way to the Louisa Colliery until 1947 when it was sent underground.

The coal from the William was also sent across to the Hedley and on up to the Louisa after the Oxhill Engine ceased working. Many years after the colliery closed, the remaining brickwork from the surface buildings were taken to Ransome & Marles Bearing Factory where they were used to make a base for the new road surrounding the large extension.

Left: The bridge which carried the coal wagons from the Hedley up to the Louisa, with a view down to Hustledown.

The Hedley Pit Heroes
An item from The London Gazette, 20th October 1931

Awards of Edward Medals, Whitehall, 5th October 1931.

His Majesty the King has been graciously pleased to award the Edward Medal to the following 19 persons in recognition of their gallantry in the circumstances mentioned below:

John Thomas Akers
Thomas Buckley
Phillip Cox
John Dart
Thomas Dixon
Charles James Brookfield Fox
Robert Johnston
James Kent
Richard Henry King
Victor King

Joseph Lens
George Forster Mason
George Nancollas
Robert Reed
Walter Robert Scott
Walter Henry Sheldrake
John George Tarn
Thomas Henry Uren
William Waugh

That on, 29th September 1930, a fall of roof occurred in the Hedley Pit, South Moor, Co Durham, partially burying a hewer, Frederick Beaumont. A chargeman, Victor King, was the first to come to the rescue. He found that a small passage way remained open by which the buried man might be reached and, with the assistance of his son Richard and John George Tarn, he immediately built two chocks of timber to keep it open. The passage was seven yards long and about two feet square, and the only practicable method of rescue was for three men to crawl along the passage way, and lie full length, two in the passage way, and one over Beaumont's body, and pass back, one at a time, the stones that were pinning him down.

This perilous and arduous work was carried on for nine hours by a team of miners working in relays under the direction of the manager, Walter Robert Scott, and under manager Robert Reed, until at last Beaumont was released, shaken, but otherwise uninjured. During the whole nine hours, the roof was shifting and 'trickling' and on four occasions, Beaumont was almost freed when a further fall buried him again. At one time, the danger of a further fall appeared so great, that the manager telephoned for Dr Charles James Brookfield Fox to come to the pit to amputate Beaumont's leg, and so expediate his release. Fortunately as it turned out, the doctor found it impossible to amputate in the restricted area in which Beaumont was confined, but he remained on the scene until Beaumont was rescued, and examined and treated him before sending him to the surface. Shortly after Beaumont was extracted, the whole of the tunnel collapsed.

The Hedley Pit Heroes.

Also, on 30th December 1931, the 19 men were awarded the Carnegie Hero Fund Certificate at West Stanley Co-operative Hall by Mr T.H. Greener. Below is a copy of one of those certificates in the name of John G. Tarn.

The men receiving their awards at the Co-operative Hall.

South Moor St John Ambulance Cadets around 1940. The officers are Laurie Hardy (left) and Bill Younger (right). Bill Younger was awarded the Edward Medal for his part in rescue work at the time of the Louisa Morrison Colliery Explosion.

Pictured at Quaking Houses with trophies. After the closure of the colliery, the old canteen at the William Pit became a Welfare Hall and was used for bingo, weddings etc. It was used in the 1970s for Holmside & South Moor Modernaires Juvenile Jazz Band for practices.

South Moor Lodge No 2 Band and Banner at South Moor Park in the 1950s.

A few Moor Band members at Tantobie after the war ended. Including: Bob Dodds, Ned Morton and Tom Stalker.

No 1 Lodge band and banner in South Moor Park around the 1950s.

Above and below: Two photographs of South Moor Band. I have no details to go with the photos. Do you know where, when and who?

Norman Tallentyre at Lanchester. He was a percussionist with South Moor for over 15 years. He worked as a rope splicer at the Morrison Busty Colliery. Apart from South Moor, he played at Newcastle Theatre Royal and Empire. He also played at local dance bands and Stanley Orchestra. When he was younger he played for the famous St Hilda's Band.

94

Pit ponies were used in most of our local coal mines and were a true asset for the hard work they performed. Over the years I have heard varying stories of good ponies, average ponies and really wicked ponies, some of who's actions resulted in deaths in the pit. Likewise, I have heard of some miners who loved their ponies and of others who were outright cruel in their handling underground. Pictured here are ponies at South Moor Hedley Pit. I have others in my collection.

Mr Dixon and Golightly with a pony at the Hedley Pit. The writing on the tub says: 'Plenty coal for the man who burst the pipe.'

Tanfield Railway

This railway is the oldest existing railway in the world. The construction of the Tanfield Waggonway southwards from Sunniside to Causey was started in 1725. The actual length of the line was from Redeugh Engine to Tanfield Moor Colliery at White-le-Head, as shown on the map. A second record is the nearby Causey Arch which is believed to be the oldest known single span railway bridge in the country. Yet a further nearby record breaking business is Hunter's of Tantobie, bus route from Stanley to White-le-Head. It is the longest continuous trading bus route in the world. Within two miles of the Tanfield Railway is the world famous Beamish Open Air Museum. You could spend a great time here in this area. The Tanfield Railway offers a good day out for the family with a look into the past, and see how steam really was a powerful form of transport.

Also on this site are the Marley Hill Locomotive Workshops which are still operating. Since restoration, they have acquired many steam engines and a selection of rolling stock. In those early days, there was great competition between the coal owners, and their need to get the coal down to the River Tyne caused many arguments and disputes. It was this that decided them to build the Tanfield Railway from 1723, by the Liddell, Wortley Group to Blackburn Fell near Sunniside, so as to avoid using the 1699 Dunston Way. The new section reached Sunniside by 1724. Liddell and Wortley were joined by Cotesworth as the way was extended to Causey in 1725. In 1726, George Bowes and others joined to form what was known as 'The Grand Allies', intending to control the coal trade for their own profit. The layout of the land caused great problems, but clever engineering overcame this, and the line was considered a great achievement. The different forms of haulage are shown on the map below, such as stationary engines, self acting inclines and horse drawn wagons.

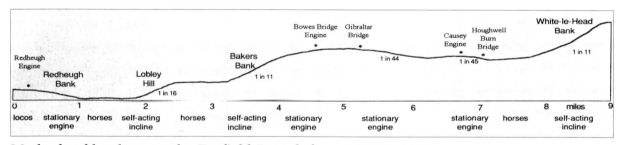

Methods of haulage on the Tanfield Branch from 1839 to 1881.

NEWCASTLE on TYNE.
showing the Brandling Junction Railway.

A sketch of coal wagons on the Gateshead side of the Tyne by Thomas Henry Hair.

Here are three photographs of Tanfield Railway.

Right: Sunniside Station.

Above: Opening day at East Tanfield.

Left: Andrews House Station in 1991.

A Selection of Mining Poetry

As I come to the end of this book, I need to mention that it has been obvious that I have highlighted the huge cost paid in the quest for coal. The industry has long gone, and for years we were left with the scars of pit heaps, old collieries etc. However, in recent years, a lot of progress has been made in most of the area. New housing estates are replacing old. Community Centres such as the one at Quaking Houses and also at Craghead. Some road improvements, and a general tidying up of the area. It can't be forgotten either that we have beautiful countryside all around us.

Considering that for some years the area was threatened with Category "D", virtually a death sentence on all new building, which was vigorously fought off, much progress has been made. Each area has formed partnerships with the local authority to take the district forward. There is still much to do, but there is now visible evidence of change. I would like to give evidence of this with Craghead village. They established a Development Trust, and through determination and sheer doggedness, they have moved mountains to make the necessary changes in the area, so as to make all things possible. New housing projects are happening all over the area. Similar things are being carried out at Quaking Houses, South Moor, New Kyo and Tanfield Lea. It won't all change over night, but it is changing. All credit to those brave enough to take the harsh decisions needed to move forward.

At Craghead, they have their own newspaper named "Canny Crack". In the March 2009 issue are two poems concerning the coal industry. I liked them so much, I asked their permission to place them in this book, as follows:

"When You Speak Of Heroes"

They have no "Workers Playtime", no music while you work
Theirs is not but long hard labour that all but heroes shirk
Yes, a miner is a hero, and should any doubt my word
Let me mention just one danger, though of many you have heard

Have you ever lain in a confined space with a constant water flow
A broken roof above you, a sodden floor below
Heard the voice of torture strata as the earth gives threatening growls
To the puny helpless humans hacking at her bowels?

Have you ever sat in the gleam of a lamp and heard timbers creek
Like hinges on the gates of Hell, and you dared not move or speak?
Have you watched a comrade dying, as stones have crushed his frame
Praying for sunlight he'll never see again

Yes it is easy to die with the sun in your face
While the gifts of God surround you
Than to die all alone in slime and dust without a friend beside you

So when you speak of heroes, and speak of them with pride
Give some thought to the miner, and how many of them died
They have no place in history, no glory in their deeds
But Britain gained a national pride, because of men like these

100 Years of Coal Black (Face)

When I was a lad, knee high to his Dad
He looked down and said to me
"Twill not be long our Jack, a miner's boy you'll be"
I looked up at the wheels a turning round
Not really knowing what lay under the ground
I know he went clean and came back black
And me mam on her knees scrubbing his back.

The years rolled by, the wheels still turning
The coals still there for the want of burning
Me Dad's not here now, he's under the ground
Not working, but resting as the wheels go round
He would have been proud to be here with me
For tis the Pit's Centenary

There's been many a struggle and a couple of strikes
Disputes, stoppages, breakdowns, the likes
But the flags flying high, the wheels a turning
The coal is still there for the want of burning
Now "I" look at my lad, knee high to his Dad
And ruffle his hair with glee
There's no doubt about it, in fact I'll be proud of it
"A miner's boy you'll be."

Jonty Lambert, my great-grandfather. He is
pictured at his home in Kettledrum Street,
Gas House Square in 1909.

99

The Price Of Coal
By Bill Norton

This was the winning poem in a poetry competition sponsored by Jack Hair in memory of his Dad, William Marsden Hair, a lifetime coal miner, to mark the occasion of West Stanley Colliery Disaster Centenary, 1909-2009.

Wor Geordie kisses his wife goodbye
And sets off for the pit
A three mile walk to get to work
Along a road ill-lit
Then lowered down 600 feet
Inside that dismal shaft
With puny little carbide lamps
To start twelve hours graft

Conditions they were worse than Hell
Seams twenty inches high
With water seeping everywhere
A stinking place to die
Pit owners didn't give a stuff
About those dread conditions
So long as coal kept coming up
They raked in their commissions

The men, they grafted every day
Sweat mingled with the dust
There wasn't any other way
For them to earn a crust
The mines extracted dreadful toll
Death was a fact of life
With miners killed most every week
Meant many a distraught wife

But nothing could prepare for this
Unearthly rumbling sound
A mighty rush of red hot air
Explosion underground
A blinding flash ripped through the mine
Right through that god damned pit
Most of the men were killed outright
Like atoms had been split

Rescuers were on the scene
In minutes they were there
They dug down for two solid days
Confusion everywhere
So few survivors from that pit
Just thirty men in all
Grim work to bring the bodies up
For one last sad roll call

In a time of such despair
It's strange what brings relief
Six pit ponies brought out alive
It just defies belief
It's sad how this disaster site
Where many met their fate
Is now largely forgotten
Neath a council house estate.

The Colliery Welfare

Most collieries had a Welfare Hall or Sports Ground. There were some excellent football and cricket teams. East Stanley was one example. It was known as Beamish & East Tanfield Welfare Ground and had a cricket pitch, football pitch, bowling green, tennis courts and play areas. When they first started, my own family on my father's side were heavily involved. They helped others lay the cricket pitch, and for their first game, they played No Place Welfare. The cricket square was not completed, so they played on a wooden wicket. Beamish & East Tanfield batted first and were bowled out for a very low score, something like 14 all out. They were very disheartened, until they bowled No Place out for even less. At the time, my father, and two of his brothers were in the team, another brother was umpire, and my grandmother and two of the daughters made the teas. A truly family affair.

Each summer, there would be the Welfare Sports Day. There were races of all kinds for the different age groups, and a picnic lunch bag for each child. Quoits was the big game for the men, quite often with side bets on the winner. At the end of the day, all those who had won or came in the first three of their event received an envelope with money in it. This was a great day out for all the family.

Tanfield Lea had their own Welfare Hall and Park. South Moor still have their cricket field while Craghead had a sports ground for cricket, football and bowls, as did most of the rest of the area.

Welfare Sports Day at Craghead.

Craghead Welfare football team in the 1940s.

A bowls game at Tanfield Lea Welfare Park.

The Disgrace of Coal and Stone Dust

Over the years, the NCB ran a scheme of x-rays on coal mineworkers regarding pneumonoconiosis and silicosis. Quite often, this involved mobile x-ray machines arriving at the collieries. The results of these x-rays determined what level, if any the miners had of coal and stone dust. Compensation awards were determined on the amount shown on the x-rays. I don't know the exact figures, but that is not important, but I believe any reading under 5% did not qualify for compensation. Also, I do not have any of the statistics to show just how many qualified. Once again, that is not an issue. My upset is with the number of relatives and miners I have spoken to concerning the results of the original x-rays.

Quite a few of those who were told they had less than 5%, eventually, in later life, discovered as the result of operations or medical conditions, found they had excessively high readings regarding the coal and stone dust. Once again, I admit I have no medical experience whatsoever. However, I do know they more than likely did not get the disease in the coal house. If they were diagnosed as less than 5% previously, then that figure could not have worsened of its own accord. Coal and stone dust does not multiply in quantity in the lungs of its own accord.

If the original findings were incorrect, and it seems on many occasions this was in fact so, who authorised the results? Was it deliberate so as to avoid compensation? Was it negligence on behalf of those who took the x-rays? Was it negligence on behalf of those who read the x-rays? Was it a genuine mistake or was it deliberate? I give the benefit of the doubt to those responsible, and ask anyone involved with this programme, still alive to give some form of explanation. I will guarantee their explanation will receive public space in the press. I will even debate the subject in public at any time or place. Former miners and their families are also invited to contact me on this subject.

Was your husband or relative wrongly diagnosed? If so, by how much? Did they die as the result of their condition? Were they awarded back payment? Are you a miner still living and suffering as the result of these misreadings? Please contact me if you are. My contact address is jackhair@tiscali.co.uk

In recent years, the NCB have offered token payments to the ageing former employees of the mining industry. This seems good, but it cancels miners and their relatives from any subsequent compensation on finding at a later date the condition was indeed much worse than originally thought to be. I believe, if the hospital can show the individual had originally been under diagnosed, then back payment should still be allowed, even at this late stage.

If you have sat with a relative suffering from either of these conditions, watching them virtually choke on coal or stone dust, and fighting for every breath of air, you will know what I am talking about, and I believe there are many of you out there. It's not only those who were told their readings were too low. Many others were told they had 10% or other low readings. Even though they claimed a lifetime pension, many of these were later found to have 80, 90 or even 100%. How could this be? Surely someone can give an acceptable explanation. If not, then I again ask the question, was it a genuine mistake or was it deliberate?

Last year, I sat with my dying father for several months in hospital. He was one of those wrongly diagnosed all those years ago. I can still feel myself trying to breath air into his lungs. Some years previous, he had an operation which meant opening up his chest. The doctors then said they had to divert to avoid the coal and stone dust. On his final visit last year, we were called in by his specialist, who told us his lungs were full of coal and stone dust. We said we were aware of this and so was my father. When he eventually died, what I can only describe as a horrible death, the Coroner refused to sign the death certificate without a Post Mortem. We explained my father did not want one and neither did we. We explained the original diagnosis of less than 5% and that we did not want to take it any further. My mother was also at this time deceased, so there would be no financial gain in any such post mortem. The Coroner was sympathetic to our wishes and allowed the body to be freed for cremation without further distress to our family. Many of you must have had similar situations. It's not nice, is it?